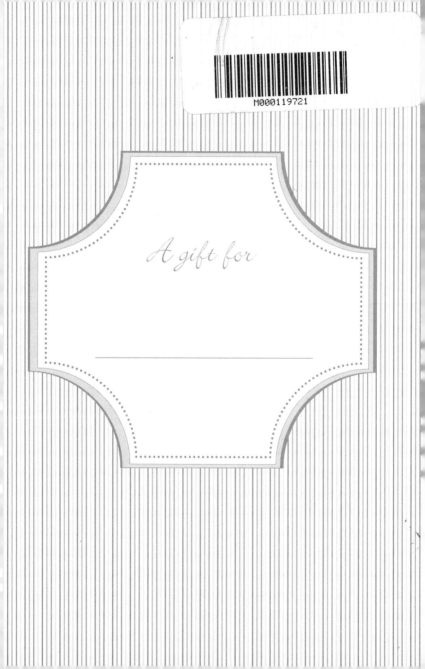

A gift for

_____

What People Are Saying About Toni S. Poynter

Author of *Now and Forever: Advice for a Strong Marriage*

"Toni Poynter is a warm-hearted philosopher with a sense of humor and an upbeat message for people who care about their marriages."

—LETITIA BALDRIGE, author on manners

"An inspiring and insightful book that will help any couple navigate through the path of their relationship."

—BARBARA DE ANGELIS, PH.D.

"The most intelligent meditation book I've encountered. Poynter's quotations are as wide-ranging as they are thought-provoking. A compassionate reminder to help couples stay connected."

—JENNIFER LOUDEN, author of *The Couple's Comfort Book*

"This is an enchantingly wise and wonderful and galvanizing book from which small secrets and large epiphanies are gleaned. From the time the author orders her husband to 'Do something with those potatoes!'—and he begins to juggle them, I was hooked. I'm so glad I read it and I wish I'd written it."

—SHERRY SUIB COHEN, author of *Secrets of a Very Good Marriage*

"Beautifully written and deeply personal, this is a map to an often difficult transition. Toni Poynter has put her heart and soul into this journey. These wise words can deepen any relationship."

—GAY AND KATHLYN HENDRICKS, coauthors of *Conscious Loving*

"This book should be read by *all* married people. Newlyweds should use it as a guidebook and those long married can use it to reawaken the spark that brought them together.

—MARK A. BRYAN, coauthor of *The Artist's Way at Work*

"*Now and Forever* touched me deeply by its quiet wisdom and sense of spaciousness about the sacred container we call marriage. I immediately decided to send it as a gift to my married children and friends."

—CAROL ADRIENNE, PH.D., author of *When Life Changes or You Wish It Would*

"Every couple seeking a beautiful life together should keep this exceptionally wise book on both sides of their bed."

—ALEXANDRA STODDARD, author of *Choosing Happiness*

Now and
Forever

*Advice for a
strong marriage*

Toni S. Poynter

LOYOLAPRESS.

CHICAGO

LOYOLAPRESS.

3441 N. ASHLAND AVENUE
CHICAGO, ILLINOIS 60657
(800) 621-1008
WWW.LOYOLABOOKS.ORG

This book is a revised and reedited edition of *From This Day Forward: Meditations on the First Years of Marriage,* published in 1995 by HarperSanFrancisco as a hardcover and in 1998 by Andrews McMeel as a paperback, and of *From This Day Forward: Inspirations for Couples*, published in 2001 by Hallmark Gift Books/HarperCollins Publishers.

The Scripture quotations contained herein are from the King James Version of the Bible.

Illustrations by Valerie Hamill Cohen
Interior design by Megan Duffy Rostan

Library of Congress Cataloging-in-Publication Data
Poynter, Toni Sciarra.
  Now and forever : advice for a strong marriage / Toni S. Poynter.
    p. cm.
Rev. ed. of: From this day forward. 1995.
  ISBN 0-8294-1932-2
  1. Marriage—Religious aspects—Christianity—Meditations. I.
Poynter, Toni Sciarra. From this day forward. II. Title.
BV4596.M3P68 2004
242'.644—dc22

                  2003020984

Printed in the United States of America
04 05 06 07 08 09 10 M-V 10 9 8 7 6 5 4 3 2 1

For my husband Donald
and
In loving memory of Eddie Maundrell,
who brought us together

Acknowledgments

While writing is a solo process, in truth a book is never written alone. Thanks go to all those whose insights during interviews were cogent, thoughtful, and laced with humor and with their own unique grace, as well as to all those whose casual comments got me thinking and helped me through many times when I feared my well of marital wisdom had run dry.

For the help you gave and for the help you didn't know you were giving, special thanks go to Mackenzie Anderson, Dana Hemmenway, Anthony "A. J." Jackson, Eric Marcus, "Mo" Matthews, Dona Munker, Sarah Rutta, Fern Sanford, and Bob Shuman. Thanks to George Luthringer, who offered divine inspiration and who has taught me from my teen years to trust my thoughts and voice.

To my family and friends, thank you for your enthusiasm and lively interest. You have no idea how much your question, "How's the book going?" actually helped it to "go"!

To my agent, Denise Marcil, thank you for being the first to catch on to my bashful idea, and for your encouragement, confidence, and friendship every step of the way over the lives this book has enjoyed.

Thanks to Joe Durepos, my editor at Loyola Press, whose astute perceptions and appreciation of what I had written helped me shape and appreciate it anew.

Finally, I thank my husband, Donald, who pushed me out of bed each morning, urging, "Go write epiphanies," who never asked me to change what I wrote about him, and who is my partner for life. Don't worry, sweetheart—I didn't tell anyone that you hang your underwear on the doorknob.

Before You Begin This Book

This book began in the realm of my own experience—I wrote the book I needed to buy—so even though I was proud of what I had done, I certainly never presumed to have the corner on any great truths about marriage. Nor, some eleven years later as this book enters its fourth edition, do I presume to know more than I did when I first rolled out of bed an hour early to start what would be the first of many mornings of reflecting and writing on the art and craft of the working marriage. What I do know is that I missed those quiet, meditative mornings after the manuscript had been written and delivered. I realized that the simple act of thinking—even for just a few minutes a day—about what it means to be in relationship to another made me more conscious of the kind of marriage I was making each day. It was an awareness that I carried not as a weight, but as wings to help lift me toward the person I wanted to be in my marriage, helping me gain some distance from the places where I tended to get stuck. I hope that by reading this book you will enjoy a similar experience of greater union with yourself and with the truest expression of your intentions in your union with another.

This book comes with no rules about how to read or experience it. It's a bit like marriage in that regard! Do what works for you. Dip into it at will. Visit the entries and find one that suits your mood. Try on several for size; let them incubate in the back of your mind as you go about your day.

Of course, you can also start at page 1 and keep going! This process is for you. The last thing we need in our busy lives is another task that feels arduous. These thoughts are meant to be enjoyed, pondered, smiled at, and shared—maybe with your spouse, maybe with a friend.

Most of all, allow yourself time for reflection. Make a space for yourself where you can nurture ideas, insights, and impressions about who you are and who you are becoming on this journey of marriage. I hope you will receive the meditations that follow in the spirit in which they are offered: as the musings of a fellow traveler.

Trinity

Such is the force of Happiness—The Least can lift a
Ton—Assisted by its stimulus.

Emily Dickinson, "No. 787"

Marriage is an entity. It is a "third thing" made up of the
two of you but also greater than the sum of your parts.
That's why, when you are really feeling in love and
connected, you get a powerful surge of energy, a sense of
everything being possible. That is the power of the "third
thing" working in you, lifting you out of yourselves, making
the two of you greater than each of you is alone. This
transformation is the real miracle of marriage. The two of you
have created something bigger than you are. Then, having
given it life, you find it becomes your life force, infusing you
with strength you never had and calling from you a wisdom
you never thought you possessed. It impels you toward a level
of greatness. It demands the best. No wonder it is so heady—
and so hard!

**In its relentless push toward the apex of our capabilities,
marriage can be the ultimate ecstatic experience.**

Take What You Need

Come unto me, all ye that labor and are heavy
laden, and I will give you rest.

Matthew 11:28

Your marriage is a place of solace. Return to it often for renewal and sustenance. It will become more and more bountiful the more you take from it. Come home and tell your partner, "I'm so glad to see you. I missed you today." Or, sitting together in the evening, "I need to lean on you." Or, "All I wanted to do all day was to be here, like this, with you." This kind of taking doesn't deplete your marriage; it fills it up with the security of knowing that both of you drink deeply from one well. The more you seek, the more your partner will have and want to give. And the safer your mate will feel to seek the same from you.

Seek renewal from your marriage. The more you take, the more will be provided for you.

Being Reborn

We were as twinn'd lambs that did frisk i' the sun,
And bleat the one at the other: what we chang'd
Was innocence for innocence.

William Shakespeare, *The Winter's Tale*

When my husband and I announced our engagement, my father said, "Good. Now you can get on with your life." I realized later that Dad had put his finger on precisely the hanging-in-the-balance sensation that both my husband and I had been feeling for months. Our unresolved future, unspoken of, had interfered with necessary life decisions. Was he going to move to the West Coast in search of work and leave me in New York, struggling with a long-distance, uncommitted relationship? Was I going to buy an apartment in an area of town where I knew he didn't want to live? Our lives were on hold until the essential "Is it me or is it we?" question got answered. Deciding to marry placed us on a new track immediately. Our lives no longer ran parallel; they were on one and the same rail.

Marriage begins a life composed of the old yet poised for the new. It asks you to be again like an infant, wondering and small.

Taking the Plunge

It matters not how a man dies, but how he lives.

Samuel Johnson, from *Boswell's Life of Johnson*

My mother married when she was eighteen—so young her parents had to give permission for the wedding to take place. The war had accelerated everything. My father was going overseas in three months. Nowadays, there tend to be fewer such sweeping forces at work to compel two people to leap into the unknown of marriage. There is only the force of our own desire, self-generated and self-accelerated, to push us toward union. No wonder marriage feels like free fall: We have left a familiar, safe place for the limitless space of the new. No one ever feels truly ready to do that.

Feeling uncertain or fearful about the future doesn't mean that you're unequal to the journey you have undertaken. It's natural to have doubts when you take on a challenge you have never before attempted. It's natural to fear stepping into the void.

Those who freely choose their path do so with deep knowledge of risk.

Be Odd

All the world is queer save me and thee; and sometimes I think thee is a little queer.

Attributed to a Quaker, speaking to his wife

Be prepared for people to judge the decisions you make in your marriage. Let them say whatever they've got a mind to; raise their eyebrows; sigh and shrug. It doesn't matter. Your marriage has to feel good only to you. It doesn't have to look good to anyone. The sooner you start tuning in to what you need in your marriage rather than to what others need it to be, the sooner your marriage will grow to be a genuine reflection of the vision and dreams of its two creators—you and your mate. And it will fit you like a glove.

All marriages are strange. Let yours work in its own strange way.

Venture Forth

It is a rough road that leads to the heights
of greatness.

Seneca, *Epistles*

Millions of people do a rare and brave thing. They leap into marriage, a totally unknown terrain. You are one of them. Expect to be confused, fearful, and sometimes lost. If you knew where you were going, you wouldn't be the explorer you are. It's tempting, during our journey, to stay on a well-cut path. But since we are not traveling alone, our path is not only up to us. Our companion may want to try detours or shortcuts—and sometimes may stop and sit down, refusing to budge.

When you embark on marriage, a journey is promised. That it will be uneventful is not part of the agreement. Your task is not to make the trip without incident, but to surmount inevitable roadblocks and come out together on the other side.

Making a smooth path in marriage is not your responsibility. The courage to embark and the strength to continue is where your effort must go.

Transformation

With this Ring I thee wed.

The Book of Common Prayer, "Solemnization of Matrimony"

One of the most disorienting things about getting married was that I didn't feel transformed after the ceremony. I had expected (and hoped) to feel wiser, more enlightened about what lay ahead. Instead, we sat in the rented limo, holding hands and saying, "We did it!" as though what had taken place had not quite penetrated us.

It had, but so deeply and subtly that we didn't notice at first. Perhaps that's why so many cultures celebrate marriage with intense ritual. You need the line of demarcation of a new life clearly and deeply drawn. It takes a while to realize that although no special wisdom or other observable virtue was conferred along with the marriage blessing, the two of you are irrevocably embarked on a journey unprecedented in your life. That's why we need the marriage ceremony: to set in motion the tectonic shifts within.

Marriage is a transformation of our spirit. In this way, it's truly a sacrament: an outward and visible sign of an inward and spiritual grace.

Defining Partnership

The greatest thing in the world is to know how to
belong to oneself.

Michel Eyquem de Montaigne, *The Essays*

When you marry, people's assumptions about "coupledom"
kick in full force. Some will expect the two of you to be
practically joined at the hip, rarely making plans apart. Others
will complain if you don't spend enough time with them, separate from your spouse. This dilemma hits at the root question of
who you are separately and together in your marriage.

You and your partner have your own expectations about
your partnership. Perhaps one of you insists on time alone with
friends and the other feels left out. The balance here must
change as your needs change. If too much separate socializing
is going on, perhaps one of you is feeling overwhelmed by the
"together forever" aspects of marriage. If your friends never see
you apart from each other, perhaps you need to consider why it
seems so important to appear as a couple.

**Like planets, you revolve around each other in distinct
but related orbits. Finding the balance that keeps you
together but separate is a delicate process.**

The Main Event

A clear fire, a clean hearth, and the rigour
of the game.

Charles Lamb, *Essays of Elia* (1823), "Mrs. Battle's Opinions on Whist"

Marriage is different from living together, a friend of mine observed, because "everyone relaxes." Often we take that to mean negative things: Both of you drop your best behavior and start to show your bad habits. That certainly happens! But it's also true that once you relax, you become more real, more genuine in every respect. More of you is available for your partner to learn about and wonder at. The tense longings and bottomless expectations of courtship fall away. You have gotten what you wanted. Now, no longer "wishing," you're "doing." A hardy, lusty realism replaces wide-eyed wonder. You get loose, ready for anything. You're an athlete, tuned up for the main event.

The familiarity and certainty that come with marriage bring strength for the journey ahead.

Your Past, Your Present

Yours for the unshackled exercise of every faculty
by every human being.

Lydia Maria Child, Message to women suffrage supporters (c. 1875)

The consuming passion to get a new marriage off on the
right foot can exhibit itself in an intense period of nest-
ing, during which you forgo many activities you pursued as a
single person. This is natural. Your energies are being poured
into creating your identity as a couple. You may have gone
too far if you find yourself thinking, *It's been so long since I*
_____. Part of the task of marriage is to integrate your past
life with your present one, not throw your former self
overboard. Selecting and slowly introducing activities and
habits you pursued in your single years is part of forging the
union of two separate souls. It is a workmanlike process, not
without friction. The reward, though, is a seamless, fluid
ability to move back and forth between your old and new
selves that is immeasurably rich.

**The person you were and the person you are must come
together in marriage. Otherwise, you will feel dislocated
within it.**

Lip Service

Anyone can hold the helm when the sea is calm.

Publilius Syrus, Maxim 358

I used to think that being supportive meant always being approving and laudatory. Now I know that it has more to do with truth telling than with praise giving. I am the only person who can tell my husband when he's full of #%&@—and survive the process. He trusts that I won't insult his intelligence by compliantly telling him what he wants to hear, but will honor him with what he needs to hear.

Confronting is a good thing, when it is done lovingly. The other person must sense your wish to help handle a bad situation, not to inflict hurt or to vindicate yourself at the other's expense.

Few people care enough about us to risk telling us the unvarnished truth when we least want to listen—and when it would most help us to hear it. Put your love in the service of honesty.

The Blessing of Being Known

Of all mad matches never was the like.

William Shakespeare, *The Taming of the Shrew*

Settle down," my husband chides during one of my fits of temper. Miraculously, I do. Anyone else telling me to "settle down" would be struck dead in his tracks. But my husband says it with such understanding that he gets away with it.

No one can rile me like my husband, but no one else can calm me as he does, either. It is a blessing to have a partner who has the courage to stand in the path of our rages and hold us in the storm of our tears. It is a blessing to find someone who has the mettle to meet us squarely on every level of who we are.

Isn't it amazing how well you know how to handle each other? Isn't it interesting that you allow each other to do so?

How You Dreamed It Would Be

The glory and the freshness of a dream.

William Wordsworth, "Ode: Intimations of Immortality from Recollections of Early Childhood"

We begin marriage filled with dreams. In fact, there is only the dream at first. Then the reality of marriage consumes us, and it's easy to get lost in the maze of day-to-day busyness, losing sight of the ideals we held at the start. Take time to remember your dreams and aspirations. Knowing them, how would you shape the details of your daily life? Without dreams, marriage becomes a collection of grunts and groans; a scrapbook of grievances; a formless space.

Recall the hopes that birthed your life together. Use them to help you place your hand wisely in the midst of conflict.

Chosen

Let each man think himself an act of God,
His mind a thought, his life a breath of God.

Philip James Bailey, *Festus* (1839), *Proem*

There's a sense of awe that this person really wants to hang out with you," a friend observed about her marriage. Just as you have chosen your spouse, so your spouse has chosen you. Remembering what an honor this is can help you to remain worthy of having been chosen. The exact reasons why you have been chosen will always remain something of a mystery— who can truly untangle the web of physical attraction, intellectual allure, and raw emotional need that causes one person to desire another? This essential mystery is good. It keeps us honing all our angles, shining all our surfaces—for who knows which facets we can afford to let dull?

Let the mystery of your partner's attraction to you spur you to be your best self.

Much Is Asked; Much Is Given

When you first were married, your ring looked so obvious and new. Now it's as if you've grown into your ring and your ring has grown into you.

A friend

Marriage calls for every ounce of maturity we have. It also offers a stage for every childish mood and tantrum. Don't be surprised if you find yourself seesawing through these emotions, feeling a wonderful calm unity one moment and the chaotic urge to scream and slam doors the next. Marriage challenges you to put into play everything you know. It demands every survival skill you possess—and many you don't yet possess. Growing into your marriage is an exhilarating challenge to the spirit.

You have taken on a large and noble task. You own it, and it owns you. You can never be shaken loose from the transformation that has occurred.

Consideration

Never . . . be mean in anything; never be false;
never be cruel.

Charles Dickens, *David Copperfield*

Recently my husband came home several hours after I had expected him. I had long since passed through puzzlement, peevishness, fury, and worry and had entered a state of pure anxiety. Seeing my wild expression, he looked sheepish. "I was in a bookstore and lost track of time," he confessed.

There is a basic level of courtesy in marriage that often must be learned through situations much like this one. Letting the other person know where you are or that you're running late smooths the path of marriage. Courtesy shows us that we are valued, thought about, and cared for.

Courtesies are a simple way to let others know how much their happiness means to us.

The Work of Time

Surely these things lie on the knees of the gods.

Homer, *The Odyssey*

When I first began dating my husband, our arguments always had to be settled right away—within hours—or I'd suffer great worry and impatience. After we'd been dating a year or so, the time frame lengthened. We sometimes took days to settle things. Now that we're married, our sense of time seems to have expanded again. I don't think of our arguments as crises that must be resolved. I think of our life as an unfolding process.

Marriage changes our notion of time. We have a lifetime to spend together—and we begin to realize that not everything can be handled quickly and decisively. Agreements are struck; then they mutate; then they are re-formed in yet another configuration as time and life re-form us. Some issues we let go of altogether. Some arise that would have been unimaginable a few years earlier. Some never get resolved.

Letting problems go unsolved doesn't mean you're getting lazy. You've learned that some problems untangle only in their own time.

Disciples

What you don't know would make a great book.

Sydney Smith, *Lady Holland's Memoir*

You have many things to teach each other. I'm talking not about philosophy here but actual skills: how to roast a chicken, shoot baskets, secure a loan, tend a campfire. Let yourselves be beginners with each other, absorbing new skills the other can teach. There is a wonderful intimacy in surrendering to each other's strengths, tapping one another's unique wisdom.

Become learners again. Honor each other with the attentive openness of the student.

Separation

We must have richness of soul.

Antiphanes, *Greek Comic Fragments*

It's important to put some air into the marriage. That means getting away from each other now and then. For some people, a night out alone or with friends does the trick. For some, it takes a week of solo camping in Colorado or museuming in London. Others may think this is strange at best; a sign of trouble at worst. As long as you both agree that nothing of the kind is afoot, what does it matter what anyone else thinks? Missing each other and coming home with stories to share enables you to meet and fall in love all over again.

In the calm space of solitude, the impetus for union is rediscovered.

Changing Each Other

Even if you persuade me, you won't persuade me.

Aristophanes, *Plutus*

I don't care. I will never care. And I don't care that I don't care!" Thus my response to my husband's pleas to sort the laundry into whites and colors. My husband feels this way about a number of equally reasonable things I'd like him to do. The lesson here is that some things we absolutely, positively will not change. Sometimes we just do what we do, and to hell with anyone else's opinion. Change can happen only with our permission. We don't change for other people. We change for ourselves. If your partner changes only to please you, you'll be resented for it. You won't have "won" a thing—you'll just think you have.

**Don't waste time trying to get each other to change.
Battle over the "biggies" if you have to, but let most of it go. Change, if it's going to happen, will take its own time.**

Friends

The people people have for friends
Your common sense appall,
But the people people marry
Are the queerest folk of all.

Charlotte Perkins Gilman, "Queer People"

You do not always have to like each other's friends. You also do not have to tell each other so. You both know the ones you're lukewarm about. Remember that you're spending your lives with each other, not with each other's friends. Instead of looking at the flaws in your partner's choice of friends, look at what choosing you says about your partner's strengths.

In our selection of others, we show many of our own qualities. In choosing you, what has your partner revealed?

Single Friends

True friendship is never serene.

Marie de Rabutin-Chantal, Marquise de Sévigné, *Letters*,
"Madame de Grignon"

Once you marry, some of your single friends may find it hard to be around you. It may be painful for them to see you happy with your mate. Perhaps it reminds them of longed-for intimacy that they do not have. You'll find it difficult to connect with them, and this will distress you. Recognize that they must come to terms with your marriage in their own time. Try to stay connected in any way you can, and try to remember that their withdrawal is more about their pain than your gain. If it happens that this friendship does not survive, understand that the parting is as sad for your friend as it is for you.

Friendships change and sometimes evaporate, with or without marriage. Acceptance may be the only path here, with the hope that it may lead, in time, to reconciliation.

What about Money?

Blame-all and Praise-all are two blockheads.

Benjamin Franklin, *Poor Richard's Almanac* (1733), February

Money, like sex, brings out interesting behavior in people. The best way to deal with the money issue is to agree to do what is fair to both of you. Otherwise, disagreements will flare or fester. Money matters need to be articulated in that evenhanded spirit: "Look, I want things to feel fair to us both." Don't let disputes ride or ignore signs of trouble. Work at them gently and carefully until you reach a resolution both of you can live with. For some, that may mean keeping everything separate and splitting expenses right down the middle. For others, it may mean merging accounts completely. For many of us, it means some middle ground between the two. Money is a murky place, where we may see our own wishes more clearly than our partner's needs—with the necessities within the marriage being murkier still.

Take money matters one step at a time. Change in this area often is incremental and must always be respectful.

Allow for Anger

We went through fire and through water.

Psalm 66:12

We're often told that we should express, express, express our anger to our partner, rooting out discords as they arise. When our anger persists, we feel we have failed. Don't expect to walk around free of anger at your partner. You know too much about each other, good and bad. You have history, good and bad. Intimacy couldn't exist without that close knowledge. If anger can't flow freely in your relationship, you will never be able to go very deep with your partner, unable to withstand the emotional pressures involved.

Instead of thinking that you and your partner must always forgive each other, why not forgive feeling angry instead? Understand that it's there because you and your partner are close, and closeness steps on toes, isn't always nice, gets messy. Let your anger teach you so it won't rule you. Let the spectrum of your marriage be big enough to hold it.

The sure way to lose Eden is to pay too much attention to the serpent. But even Eden had a serpent.

Creating Traditions

The basis of a democratic state is liberty.

Aristotle, *Politics*

Forging your own traditions is an important statement—both to yourselves and to your families. It lets everyone know that a new family exists that hadn't existed before. If your families assume that holidays will be celebrated the same as always, for example, it's up to you to make your own assertions. Be gentle and matter-of-fact and don't wait until the last minute to announce your plans. Ease your relatives into the realization that the two of you now are answerable to each other and that it's more important for you and your partner to be in accord than to try to juggle others' schedules and expectations. Do this gradually, because it helps to be humane rather than harsh and divisive—and because you may need these gentle reminders as much as others do.

Creating a new identity as a couple is an incremental process. Everyone needs time to adjust. Go slowly, but don't let others ignore the fundamental shift in priorities and accountability that has taken place.

Grown Together

So I can't live either without you or with you.

Ovid, *Amores*

One gets to this point quickly in marriage. We can't conceive of life without our partner, but the idea of spending the rest of our days with this collection of bumps, bruises, bad habits, and odd attitudes seems equally unthinkable. It is a strange position that asks us to live two mutually exclusive points of view. Somehow we rise to the occasion, which is a testament to the deep character marriage calls from us. We take the bumps because we know the goodness that lives behind them. We take and make the goodness wherever we can and live on its promise during dark days.

Marriage asks us to contemplate "forever" as a way of life. It is a world without end of our own creation.

Growth

Love knows nothing of order.

St. Jerome, Letter VII, to Chromatius, Jovinus, and Eusebius

Marriage grows jaggedly. My husband and I enjoy months of serenity, followed by weeks when every comment seems to spark an argument. It appears we must go through these periods when, like clothes we outgrow, we don't "fit" each other and must remake the mantle of our marriage. Or maybe we are like the glacier cutting through granite. We exert on each other a constant, primordial pressure, grinding a new landscape for ourselves.

Marriage is a natural force set in motion. Its growth, uneven and ill-timed, carries its own inexorable logic. When we are strong enough and ready, we are compelled to stretch, flex, and demand the room our new selves require.

Marriage changes as we change. The process is like any natural phenomenon—uneven, unpredictable, relentless. Take the surges as they come.

Being There,
Getting There

If you should put even a little on a little, and should
do this often, soon this too would become big.

Hesiod, *Works and Days*

Sitting around a picnic table with friends just after we were married, my husband and I feel like babes in the woods. One couple has been married for seventeen years. The other is working on thirty. The years pass so quickly, our friends tell us; time goes faster and faster. The clichés run past us, meaningless. Our friends have no secrets to offer, no success formulas. They don't really know how they got as far as they have, any more than we know how we'll get there. "One thing about your father," my mother once told me, "is that he's always there." Willingness counts as much as wisdom, it seems, in the enduring marriage.

Sometimes the success of the game lies in just showing up every day, ready to play.

Forgive Yourself

What soul is without flaws?

Arthur Rimbaud, "Bonheur"

You've done something wrong. Said something wrong. Things are bad, and it's your fault. Have some compassion for yourself. You can admit your mistakes without beating yourself up over them. Forgiving yourself gives you the space to acknowledge the part you played in creating the problem, and the mental freedom to invent a way out of chaos.

You do many things right each day. Remember what you did right yesterday? But you are going to make mistakes sometimes. Think of the allowances you make for your spouse's imperfect behavior. Realize that he's probably making allowances for you, too. Be strong enough to admit your faults, apologize if that's necessary, and move on.

Your marriage can tolerate a tremendous amount of strain. Have faith that it can contain your flaws. Use its elasticity as a model for self-acceptance.

Live It, Don't Watch It

No thing great is created suddenly, any more than a
bunch of grapes or a fig. If you tell me that you
desire a fig, I answer you that there must be time.
Let it first blossom, then bear fruit, then ripen.

Epictetus, *Discourses*

I used to remember every significant date related to our relationship: six months of dating; one year of dating; and so on. Wandering in a churchyard in Bailey's Island, Maine, the day after we were married, I looked at my watch at 3:20 P.M. and realized that exactly twenty-four hours earlier, we had exchanged vows.

Nowadays, I often forget these landmarks. This worried me at first. I thought I was becoming jaded. Eventually I realized that when we marry, we're on the decade plan. The landmarks are measured in thirty-year mortgages; decades until retirement; silver and golden anniversaries. When we feel secure, we aren't compelled to tally each small goal attained.

The time line of your life is unfolding on a different level now. Celebrate your new ability to meet time on expanded terms.

Peace

**As soon as you trust yourself,
you will know how to live.**

Johann Wolfgang von Goethe, *Faust*

An even keel is a tempting thing. In our relationship, we sometimes keep the peace for the sake of maintaining an ideal image—public or private. We also may do it because we're too tired, too sad, too angry to know what else to do. So we go along to get along. The result may be welcome silence in the house but a clamor within. The next time you are tempted to steer toward an even keel, first consider your *inner* silence. What would it take to achieve that? Doing what is needed to achieve internal equilibrium might be the way to achieve real peace at home.

The quality of our inner silence is the source of all our offerings in marriage. Seek the contentment your soul requires.

Comradeship

So we grew together, / Like to a double cherry,
seeming parted, / But yet an union in partition; / Two
lovely berries molded on one stem.

William Shakespeare, *A Midsummer Night's Dream*

Particularly if we've been single for a while, we have gotten very good at acting unilaterally. After all, if we didn't take care of it/decide it/do it, who would? I am always shocked, then, when I come home and trot out my latest decisive action, and my spouse not only tells me why he thinks it's a lousy decision but also demands to know why he wasn't consulted. It would be inappropriate to check in on every question. But now there is another person in the equation who is just as independent and intelligent as you are—and who wants a say in the choices affecting your lives. Collaboration can be a great comfort—if we remember to do it!

You're going to be challenged about things no one challenged you about before—but you don't have to make all the decisions alone anymore.

Relatives

Criticism comes easier than craftsmanship.

Pliny the Elder, *Natural History*

Relatives are not to be used as ammunition. They are not to use you as ammunition. You and your mate must agree on these two basic principles, or your marriage will be ruled by your ties to your family of origin instead of by your sworn bond to each other. Resist the urge to psychoanalyze your in-laws. You may not be thanked for insights it is your partner's job to learn. It also is not loving or respectful to your in-laws.

If you enjoy your in-laws, tell them so, often and whole-heartedly. If you don't enjoy your in-laws, a charitable attitude is less corrosive for all concerned. It is sad that they don't know any other way to be; that they can't experience the relief of feeling open, trusting, loving. This doesn't make their actions less infuriating, but it may help you find the compassion you need to maintain your own humanity and goodwill.

Feeling upset, suspicious, and defensive stresses you more than anyone else. Why allow anyone that power?

Tolerance

You cannot teach a crab to walk straight.

Aristophanes, *Peace*

There are some household chores my husband just won't do. He appears to have a permanent impairment when it comes to cleaning the toilet. Nor have I ever seen him voluntarily set mop to floor. But I am incurable when it comes to my habit, while cooking, of tasting as I go. And I frequently wash the dishes without my contact lenses in, resulting sometimes in a knife reposing in the drainer, one side still lacquered with peanut butter. "The legend continues," my husband sighs, sticking it back under the faucet. We all come to a point in marriage where we recognize the things our partner simply won't do—or won't stop doing. It's not about sexism, laziness, or deep flaws in character (although in the heat of the moment, I've doubted this). It's just about accepting the immutability of idiosyncrasy. Give it up, both of you. Let the other guy be.

Your partner's quirks of character are there for the duration. They really are not calculated affronts to you. Try not to take them personally.

Isolation

To know that you do not know is the best.
To pretend to know when you do not know
is a disease.

Lao-tzu, *The Way of Lao-tzu*

When it comes to marriage, lots of people have advice, but few have wisdom. It's as though, after the vows are taken, a curtain descends, and each person's experience of marriage becomes the most private of secrets. People are plenty willing to tell you what's "right" and "normal." Few, however, will admit to the dismay and confusion that marriage throws us into; the sense, at times, of floundering toward solutions. To hear of these struggles would be to hear wisdom. We know we must find our own answers; we simply seek the reassurance that others, too, struggle. Many are reluctant to admit this, yet it would be the greatest comfort to know. In this way, our culture makes islands of us all.

When we feel that everyone else is doing okay and we aren't, we become isolated and discouraged. In fact, everyone struggles, and you are not alone.

Hidden Agendas

Once harm has been done,
even a fool understands it.

Homer, *The Iliad*

My partner just can't take encouragement," a friend lamented. His statement was puzzling. Lots of people can't take criticism, but who doesn't crave encouragement? Sometimes, however, we offer our partner criticism couched in encouragement. Then we're dismayed and affronted when our partner rejects our well-meant words.

If you think you're being supportive but end up in an argument, chances are your partner has picked up a subtext: You are more focused on changing than on supporting your spouse. Somehow *your* standards have become the measure, and *your partner* has been lost in the process. Your wisdom will fall on deaf ears if it is more for your peace of mind than for your partner's. It's worth asking yourself: Why have you decided that what your partner has accomplished isn't enough?

True praise comes with no strings attached.

Doing Nothing

**That indolent but agreeable condition
of doing nothing.**

Pliny the Younger, *Letters*

Take time to hang out together—otherwise, you may forget how. In the busy world we hit headlong every day, doing nothing is a skill that needs cultivating. If you've gone for a long time without doing nothing, it will seem strange at first. You'll twitch and flit; get up and sit down; start to talk and stop again. Just sit with your restlessness and wait it out. When it passes, you'll be able to find pure companionship, free of the frenzied romantic energy of the early days before life together habituated you to each other.

Sit and do nothing together. More than talking, it will put you back in sync.

Love and Laughter

He does it with a better grace,
but I do it more natural.

William Shakespeare, *Twelfth Night*

I'm getting in with you." My husband sticks one foot into the bathwater. I start to giggle and then am speechless, fighting for air, elbow- and leg-space in our ancient bathtub, which is small enough to beach a minnow. Soon our romantic tryst is reduced to a bristle of limbs in a tepid puddle. "Fun," my husband mutters, his head wedged against the faucet.

Laughter can be a great aphrodisiac—which is a good thing, since sex can be pretty laughable. And sometimes laughter is more available than steamy ardor, especially when the days are long and hectic.

Waiting for the "perfect moment" will only keep you waiting. Take what you can get and give what you can give. Start now.

Face the Music

Give your ears, hear the sayings,
Give your heart to understand them;
It profits you to put them in your heart.

Amenemope, *The Instruction of Amenemope*

Every now and then, our partner brings us down to earth with a thud by telling us a truth about ourselves that makes us wince, squirm, deny, or counterattack. When this happens to you, ask yourself if you are reacting so powerfully because a truth you don't want to admit is being revealed about you. What is so dangerous about examining it, turning it over like a puzzle in your hands? Admitting that your partner is right needn't come until later; you've got plenty of time to batten down your pride for that. In the meantime, instead of lobbing a grenade into the enemy camp, receive your mate's comment with a sense of possibility: "That's an interesting observation. I'll need some time to think about that."

You are going to hear some tough truths about yourself in the course of your marriage. Why not use them to your advantage?

Visions and Sightings

The magic of a face.

Thomas Carew, "Epitaph of the Lady S——"

A strange thing happened today at the movies," my husband told me. "I was thinking about you, and suddenly I saw you in a whole new way. You literally looked different in my imagination. You were like someone I'd never seen before, right there in the middle of *Journey to the Center of the Earth*."

I, too, have had this experience of seeing my partner anew, almost as a stranger, compelling my interest. It's an unsettling but wonderful trick of the mind that reveals, in a sort of vision, our partner's enduring mystery. It is a reminder of the essential unknowability of the person we married. It reignites our desire to plumb this intriguing person's depths. It reminds us that complete knowledge of another hangs just out of reach, keeping us wondering. And that is just as it should be.

The more you think you know your partner, the more elusive your partner becomes. Dive deep and realize you will never touch bottom.

Skin to Skin

And now good morrow to our waking souls,
Which watch not one another out of fear;
For love, all love of other sights controls,
And makes one little room, an everywhere.

John Donne, "The Good Morrow"

In the morning, before you get up, touch each other. Let the day wait, all its busyness still before you, while you re-acquaint yourselves with each other. There's no reason to snap to attention at the call of the clock. As you swim up out of sleep, in that delicious pre-waking lethargy, make a new imprint of your lover on your body and mind. Rest and absorb the safety of your marital bed. Be cradled in the knowledge that you are beloved—a reminder of the divine mystery that you are sustained by something greater than the daily whirlwind.

Restore each other with touch.

Open Heart

And we forget because we must
And not because we will.

Matthew Arnold, "Absence"

Forgiveness doesn't mean you don't remember hurts. It is a voluntary act, undertaken despite pain. In marriage, you need sometimes to be bigger than your emotions.

Don't expect the pain and anger to go away. You must make a decision to walk away. This is not the same as burying your hurts. True forgiveness is wholehearted and does not look back. True forgiveness is a quiet voice that says, "Let us continue. Let us go on with our journey." It is far easier to crouch in your dark tent than to set your feet on this path. But there is no way to find the next oasis if you won't cross the desert.

Don't wait to feel in the mood to forgive. Take yourself in hand and set out toward the serenity you seek. Forgiveness is your choice to make.

The Promise of Pictures

From their eyelids as they glanced dripped love.

Hesiod, *The Theogony*

I should look more often at my wedding pictures. Like most people, I get them out only occasionally to show others. But every time I turn the thick pages of that album and see our happy faces, the smiles of those who love us witnessing our vows, I reconnect with the hope and passion that fuel marriage. It's all there in our faces. It is inspiring to recall that day of promises made, surrounded by those who raised us to the point where we could make them.

Your marriage photos capture you at your most solemn, your most committed, your most ecstatic. Keep them where you can treasure them often.

Helping vs. Nagging

Have I inadvertently said some evil thing?

Phocion, from *Plutarch, Apothegms*

My husband needs to lose some weight. I need to write this book. Each day we work at helping each other meet our goals. When "helping" crosses over into nagging, it only makes the other person feel inadequate and angry—like a child under the thumb of a parent—not a climate where the kinds of change that require the intelligence and persistence of maturity can occur. It also puts you in the thankless position of "doing the doing" for your partner. You aren't helping by nagging or by taking over. Instead, create a climate where change can happen. For me, this means buying fewer treats and not turning food into a stress-reducing reward for myself and my spouse. It also means *not* rationing the treats when we have them. For my husband, it means encouraging me to "go write epiphanies." It also means that he doesn't check up on whether I'm writing them or not.

Give your partner the space to do his or her own good. Then sit on your hands, bite your tongue, and celebrate every small step.

Have Fun

Nothing like a little judicious levity.

Robert Louis Stevenson, *The Wrong Box*

Spend as much time as possible laughing with your partner. Look for funniness in life and share it with each other, even during difficult times. Shared happiness is the mortar that holds your house together. Mix humor into your marriage as consciously as you mix passion, insight, and judgment. Sometimes the only thing that gets you over a rough spot is a whistle or a smile.

Laughter helps you give trouble the back of your hand. Let it lighten you.

Stay Curious

Speak to him, for there is none born wise.

Ptahhotpe, *The Maxims of Ptahhotpe*

One night I stayed late at work after two weeks of doing nothing but staying late at work. When I finally called my husband to tell him I was about to leave, it was with the knowledge that he had been expecting me more than an hour earlier. "Just come home," he said tersely. I did, filled with a noxious mixture of guilt for keeping him waiting and resentment that he was being so possessive of my time.

Not until a week later did I learn that I'd gotten it all wrong. He hadn't been angry *at* me; he'd been angry *for* me: He felt that lately I hadn't been setting aside enough time for myself. I was selling him short while seeing myself as the martyred hero. The scary thing was, if I hadn't thought to ask a simple question—"Why did you sound so angry when you said that?"—I never would have discovered his compassion.

The more convinced you are of what's going on with your partner, the less you probably know. Never underestimate the clarifying power of a direct question.

Insist on Being Indulged

whim *n* : a capricious or eccentric and often sudden idea or turn of the mind.

Webster's Collegiate Dictionary (11th edition)

"Why should I bring you flowers, when all they do is die?" This is how my husband responds when I tell him that I think it's fun to receive flowers. He may never understand my whim. I don't understand it myself, except that it has something to do with glorious color and blissful self-indulgence. Understanding your partner's whims is beside the point. The point is that *you indulge them even though you don't understand them*. Whims are unexplainable by definition! Impress upon your partner that you want to be given flowers . . . or served breakfast in bed . . . or be gifted with the latest household gadget for no other reason than that you want it. Who said that everything about us had to make sense?

Having your whims indulged signifies your lover's unconditional acceptance. Don't feel guilty about asking to have your whims met. And remember to return the favor!

Best Friends, Worst Enemies

Stand your ground. Don't fire unless fired upon, but
if they mean to have a war, let it begin here!

John Parker (to his Minutemen at Lexington, Massachusetts)

Trite as it may seem, my husband and I have become best friends. So when we argue, an odd thing happens: Because we always confide our troubles to each other, we feel unnerved and fearful when anger makes us withdraw into silence. Just when we're in the thick of not speaking to each other, we have the greatest impulse to confide in the very person with whom we're locked in combat. This urge helps drive the compulsion to make up.

When you're arguing, you'll probably use your deep knowledge of your partner as a weapon. Be sure, as well, to use all you know about his friendship to move toward reconciliation.

Your best friend is also your craftiest, most persistent enemy. This is one of the practical jokes of marriage.

Running the Same Race

At last the Dodo said, *"Everybody has won, and all must have prizes."*

Lewis Carroll, *Alice in Wonderland*

My husband is a high-energy guy: up 'til the small hours; waking the next morning bright-eyed and sharp-witted. I am slower, needful of sleep, seeking "downtime" in which to daydream and do a lot of nothing. We have had to learn to respect each other's very different ways of going about life. Expecting him to slow down and enter my misty world, or me to enter his electric one, only disorients us both. We have found that when left to our own devices, each of us ends up in the same place, starting from different points. And the insights we bring from the landscape of our peculiar journeys enrich each other beyond measure.

You are never as wise alone as you are together.

Come Clean

Truths kindle light for truths.

Lucretius, *De Rerum Natura*

Create a safe space in which your partner can tell you the truth. No one likes to be castigated in their moment of self-revelation. Creating a space for truth telling doesn't mean that you can't feel sad, agitated, or angry with your partner. It does mean that you need to practice sidestepping the knee-jerk reactions you're tempted to make when your partner summons the courage to fess up. Try to acknowledge what both of you are experiencing: "This really upsets me, but I'm glad you told me." Seeing how your reactions open the way to honesty—and realizing how good honesty feels—your partner may begin to allow you the space to do the same. That's a plus, because the best way to encourage truth telling is to do it yourself.

Make a habit of coming clean with each other. You will squirm sometimes. But the payoff in trust is huge and worth pursuing.

What It Takes

The giving of love is an education in itself.

Eleanor Roosevelt

Marriage invites us to make generosity a daily practice. It asks us to move over, emotionally and physically, to let another in. This doesn't feel comfortable. While we welcome the closeness our partner brings, we resist the demands intimacy makes on our emotions. Yet there can be no true intimacy without this deeper exposure. It's like sex the first time with anyone: One reason it's intimate is that you are naked in front of another person whose caring and approval matter desperately to you. Marriage requires you to get naked emotionally with your partner. You will feel very exposed. But there can be no deepening of the closeness between you without this gradual peeling away of your defenses. Dive into your generosity—give those layers up—and open yourself to the new territory to be explored.

Marriage opens you up very wide. It requires a bright courage. It asks you to give and give again. It is natural to struggle against it at times, for this is nothing less than a test of the spirit.

The Tyranny of Perfection

Nothing endures but change.

Heraclitus, from Diogenes Laertius, *Lives of Eminent Philosophers*

Our culture sets many standards for achievement: grades, test scores, and performance reviews. Marriage has no such landmarks. There's no way to chart progress. Anniversaries measure only length, not depth. And in marriage, depth is everything.

Marriage takes a long time and is always a work in progress. It can't ever be finished, even if one of you dies. It continues to work on you, shaping who you become. A process so broad, so powerful, cannot be measured by any terms we know. You are never "there" or "finished." Don't expect to "get it right." Getting marriage right is not the goal. Keeping it deeply alive is.

Marriage can't be graded like a test. It will not serve up its riches in a framework of right and wrong. Look for periods of turbulence framed by stretches of deep contentment. That is the measure of marriage.

Push, Pull, Partner

A companion's words of persuasion are effective.

Homer, *The Iliad*

In a working marriage, each partner pushes the other to go the extra mile. It's not really about pushing, however, so much as it is about being like athletes in a relay, passing the baton so one surges forward when the other is temporarily spent. My husband cajoles me into going to the museum one freezing Saturday night, when I would have stayed indoors swaddled in lethargy. I coax him into making a special meal rather than taking the easy way out with the same old, same old. In this way, we pull each other forward, hand over hand, with our unique energies and talents. When one of us gets tired, the other's drive carries us both; when the other hangs back, the first is revived and takes up the cause.

Notice the interplay between your energies. See how they mingle and dance, impel and ignite.

One Plus One Equals One

All's right with the world.

Robert Browning, "Songs," from *Pippa Passes*

It is our first Christmas alone together. We waken entwined against the frigid weather outside. The cat sits, purring, on our chests. We are a family: two big lumps and a little lump, huddled and happy in the safe world we have made. We are joined; we are "we." When did this happen?

Watch for signs of the family you are becoming. They will come upon you as quietly as a cat creeping for comfort; burst upon you like cold winter air. They will make you calm and reverent. They will take your breath away.

Revere the union you have created.

Tread Softly

The greatest fault of a penetrating wit is to go
beyond the mark.

François, Duc de La Rochefoucauld, *Reflections*

Sometimes you will run headlong into your partner's pain.
You may not realize it until you're blasted with reaction—
perhaps a flash of deflective anger, or stony silence. When
your partner's response seems inappropriate or out of
proportion to the situation, it's a cue that you may be
confronting very old fears or beliefs, often learned in
childhood—always learned the hard way. Use these as clues.
They are valuable opportunities, not as insights for gaining
leverage, but to see more deeply into your partner.

**Volatility is a sign that you've touched a nerve in your
partner, viewing a place that few ever see. Rather than
press your advantage, tread respectfully and ask rather
than demand. Let change unfold as your partner can
tolerate it.**

Self-Sacrifice

It is idle to play the lyre for an ass.

St. Jerome

Do you do things "for the relationship" rather than because you want to? That can lead to resentment if your good intentions aren't met with the appreciation you think they deserve. Your anger then becomes an accusation: "I did it for you!" Your mate will sense the injustice of this and naturally will go on the defensive. And down the spiral goes.

A variant of this situation occurs when a couple vows to give up habits together: to stop smoking, eat less, exercise more, and so on. It's a great idea in principle, but what happens if one person backslides and the other stays the course? Will there be annoyance, or a sense of betrayal? If so, perhaps an examination of motives is in order.

When you make a decision to take action on something, ask yourself whether you'd feel glad you did it even if your spouse didn't do it with you. That way you do not lose yourself in the marriage.

Criticism

He who would distinguish true from false must have an adequate idea of what is true and false.

Benedict Spinoza, *Ethics*

I hate being criticized. And I hear just about everything as criticism. My fat ego leaps in between me and the truth. "How come you think everything is a slight?" my husband snaps. This endless self-defense is a tough habit to break. It's hard to listen with an open mind and heart, and to consider that maybe our partner's harsh words are coming from an honest place. It's not easy to give our partner's motives the benefit of the doubt.

Before you kick sand in your partner's face, look for a grain of truth.

Exposed

And they were both naked, the man and his wife,
and were not ashamed.

Genesis 2:25

My husband knows me so well, I don't know whether to be grateful or annoyed. He blows my cover when I try to save face in an argument. He won't rise to the bait when I'm itching for a fight.

It's unnerving to have someone know us so well that none of our usual tricks work. It feels as if we have been caught naked. But as clearly as our partner can see our manipulations, so our mate can also see our pain and embrace it without even having to understand it. When my husband takes one look at me and folds me in his arms, I'm glad that, to him, I am as transparent as glass.

You can't be understood as you've always longed to be without being revealed as never before.

Thrills and Chills

Most folks are about as happy as they make up their minds to be.

Abraham Lincoln

Sex—how much, how little, how often? Here's one true thing about sex: it's never the same, and it's never only good or only bad. Sometimes it's hotter than other times. Sometimes you're having sex a lot; sometimes not much. The only time that any of this is a problem is if one of you thinks it is. The only way to know this is (you guessed it) to talk about it. When things are great, tell each other how great things are. When fatigue, hectic schedules, or crossed wires are the order of the day, tell each other that you miss one another, so both of you know that you haven't lost interest, or worse, forgotten what should be unforgettable!

Make time to rekindle. But when you have no time, have faith that the spark is there.

Whom Are You Protecting?

Anchors aweigh, my boys, / Anchors aweigh!

Alfred Hart Miles, "Anchors Aweigh"

It's frightening for us when the people we love court danger. My husband rides his bicycle all over Manhattan in snowstorms and rush-hour traffic. He's been tossed atop taxis, drenched in puddles, and sideswiped by sadistic drivers. He wears a helmet and he's a careful, confident rider, but I'm haunted by visions of disaster. Should my fears make him stop? I don't think so. He is not, after all, doing anything irresponsible or reckless. He's just doing his thing. We don't have the right to demand that people we love be less than fully who they are simply because their exuberant selves make us worried, frightened, or uncomfortable. We must let them be in the world, blessing them for who they are, not for who we'd like them to be.

It's not our partner's job to make us feel comfortable and safe, confident and cared for. Peace of mind is our responsibility.

Discomfort Zones

The easy, gentle, and sloping path . . . is not the path
of true virtue. It demands a rough and thorny road.

Michel Eyquem de Montaigne, *Essays*

Our body will do anything to maintain the status quo.
When we try too hard to lose weight, our body,
defending against starvation, slows our metabolism so we stay
at the same old hated poundage. We perspire or goose-pimple
as our body works to keep its temperature at the norm.

This drive for sameness is called homeostasis. If our body
strives for the status quo, can our nature be any different? But
emotional homeostasis can stunt our growth. When marriage
challenges us to feel more deeply, to tap reserves of strength,
skill, and understanding, we may resist with all we've got—
because we're being asked to leave the stable shores we know
so well. In every molecule, we experience this as danger.

**A profound sense of danger may be a clue that a path for
growth has opened. Rather than resist, persist. Sit with the
danger until it feels more familiar. Then go a little deeper
and sit again. And so on.**

Your Space

I had three chairs in my house: one for solitude, two
for friendship, three for society.

Henry David Thoreau, *Walden*

Carve out some space in your home that is yours alone.
Present this to your partner not as if it were negotiable
but simply as a puzzle that you must solve together: "If we put
the bureau here, where am I going to have my desk/office/
studio/reading chair?" Both of you deserve a space of your
own, where there is no trace of others' presences. Don't give
in to the temptation to merge everything just because your
lives are now yoked together. Even in the smallest living
space, a tabletop, a chair, several drawers, and a lamp can be
designated as one person's turf. You will discover that finding
the space is not nearly as hard as claiming it for your own.

**Being united in marriage does not extend to letting your
partner take over the environment so no trace of "you"
remains. State your boundaries with grace and clarity, as
many times as it takes.**

Your Handiwork

My face in thine eye, thine in mine appears.

John Donne, "The Good Morrow"

Working late one night, I called home: "How about Chinese takeout?" My husband laughed. "Funny you should ask. On the way home, I picked up a menu from that new restaurant up the street."

Relish your evolving partnership: the beautiful symmetries between you; the easy way you toss the ball of life back and forth. You may be struggling with many areas of stress, but remember that there once was a time when you didn't even know each other's middle names. Look at how far you have come in your understanding of one another.

Admire the process of partnership as it unfolds naturally between you, the result of your dedication and steadfast love.

Small Stuff/Big Stuff

The boy called, "Wolf, wolf!" and the villagers came
out to help him.

Aesop, "The Shepherd's Boy and the Wolf"

Some conflicts must be worked out. Some must be waited out. A few are serious enough that they must be handled immediately. If you treat every crisis at the same level of magnitude, your partner will stop listening when you need it the most. Who can attend, consider, and resolve with equal skill all the time? Since you are honored to have someone whose desire is to listen to you and love you, learn to weigh problems and attend to the biggest ones first. Once the "biggies" are taken care of, you may find that many smaller issues recede in importance.

**One large conflagration over the right issue clears the air
better than a dozen skirmishes around the perimeter.**

Hot Spots

The will to do, the soul to dare.

Sir Walter Scott, "The Lady of the Lake"

Every marriage has "hot spots" that neither partner wants to touch. They are usually subjects that cause deep flare-ups between you. The "hot spots" list begins to be compiled very early in courtship, when both of you start to realize the importance of the relationship, and the instinct to preserve the bond exerts its power. Sometimes these spots are so hot that we won't even admit them to ourselves, much less gather the courage to work them through with our partner.

Take some time to notice where these hot spots appear in your marriage. Practice describing them to yourself. When you forge into one, stand there quietly and take in the landscape. What does the relationship look like from that vantage point? What's so frightening about being there? What feelings are triggered by just the thought of that hot spot?

Step slowly into dangerous terrain. You will survive the experience. Venturing out is a brave thing.

A New Focus

And the combat ceased for want of combatants.

Pierre Corneille, *Le Cid*

Think about something your partner does that infuriates you. If you've found that trying to change the behavior only creates antagonism, try focusing on the *behavior* instead of the person. Ask yourself: What would it take to change this behavior? Then act in a way that is consistent with the change you seek.

When you shift your attention in this way, your language and actions will move away from attacking your partner, and toward solving the problem. Anger at your partner no longer rules you. Your partner, no longer feeling attacked, may no longer resist. Your change in focus frees your partner to do the same. Now the two of you can analyze what the behavior is doing to your relationship.

Instead of focusing on the problem, focus on the results you seek. Notice how this changes your interactions with your partner.

Participation

One would grow poor staying in one place always.

Poem of the Cid, twelfth century

I don't take for granted the fact that we're married," a woman told me. "He can leave anytime." Our partner is not like an old shoe—familiar to us in every angle and up for any trek we undertake. We tend to think in terms of whether we want to stay with our partner. But let's put the "old shoe" on the other foot: What happens if our partner decides *we* aren't wanted?

Marriage is not a right conferred upon us. We must keep ourselves worthy of it. If we are bored or annoyed, it's our responsibility to do something about it, not passively keep score of every flaw.

In marriage, you either stay or go. There is no place here for one who sits and waits.

Leave Your Lover Alone

The truly silent, who keep apart,
He is like a tree grown in a meadow.

Amenemope, *The Instruction of Amenemope*

Sometimes your partner will be sad or angry, and you won't know why. Your partner cannot be an open book to you. There are times when your partner needs to be inaccessible, quiet, and alone. All of us need refuge from time to time. We must draw into ourselves to struggle, to resolve, to renew. When your partner is doing this, respect the process and don't interfere. You'll reconvene when your partner is ready.

When your partner pulls away from you, watch quietly and stay available. Let your partner take the lead in returning to your confidence.

A Different Kindling

**I found my lover on his bed, and my heart was
sweet to excess.**

Love Songs of the New Kingdom

Remember when love between you was new: when your
lover entered a crowded room, you felt a jolt of excitement; an electric awareness of every move he or she made?
Where does that little spark go after long familiarity?

Paradoxically, time—the very thing that increases your
intimacy—evaporates this intensity. The old spark once kept
aglow by mystery now must be kindled by reverence for your
deep knowledge of each other. Who else has tended you
when you were ill, held you through terrors, stuck with you
through rages, and helped you survive disasters both imagined
and real? Your intimacy now may not have the sharp edge of
that early excitement, but its steady glow illuminates where
passion only ignites.

Why chase the spark when you have made fire?

A Danger Sign

I do desire we may be better strangers.

William Shakespeare, *As You Like It*

If passion is marriage's fuel, apathy is its poison. Even when passion is expressed in arguments, at least you care enough to fight!

When you realize that you want to give up fighting for your vision of your marriage, red flags should go up. Sound the alarm to your partner, because apathy's hand is deadly. Knowing that you both still care can pull you together on an island of common ground, however small, in the sea of differences between you.

Stay in touch with your desire to fight for your marriage. Don't confuse resignation with acceptance.

Begin Again

Behold, I stand at the door, and knock.

Revelation 3:20

Coming off a weekend filled with spats, tiffs, and tears, we tread softly around each other Monday morning. There is a healing that happens during the night that has made us forget what the arguments were about, leaving only shadows of fatigue and a wish to start over. I've come to count on this feeling as a way to root out the habit of picking up the argument midstream, hanging on to the threads of rage all through the night. Basically it's easier to connect than to fight. When the argument degenerates into the blinding desire to make one's point, the point itself is eclipsed. So this morning I cover his shoulders with the sheet, warming him, before I get up to write. He mumbles and rubs his toes against mine. We start a new day.

Pay attention to your urge to connect rather than continue the turbulence. Sometimes it's better to move on than to press your point.

Coming Attractions

**As an apple tree among the trees of the wood,
so is my beloved among the sons.**

Song of Solomon 2:3

Don't expect to stop looking at the opposite sex just because you're married. Don't expect your partner to stop, either. The opposite sex is always interesting, in all its numbers, shapes, and forms. Looking is no betrayal of your spouse; it's an expression of yourself as a curious, sexual being. Using fantasy habitually to withdraw from your partner emotionally or sexually is another matter. It's a sign that something has come between you that needs to be worked out. The object of the attraction is only a symbol of that interference. Rather than waste time arguing about that, root out the deeper problem and you'll be getting closer to the truths that need expression.

Interest in others is not the problem. Lack of interest in each other is.

Why You Fell in Love

I both love and do not love,
and am mad and am not mad.

Anacreon, "Fragment 79"

One evening, rushing to put dinner on the table, I ordered my husband, "Do something with those potatoes!" He started to juggle them. Not what I had in mind, but effective at getting me to laugh and let go of my bad day.

My husband's screwball spontaneity, disarming wit, and exuberance make him eternally interesting. They also contribute to his infallible talent for losing phone numbers; his penchant for leaving the ice-cream container open on the kitchen table while he dashes away to catch something on TV; his habit of not fitting into my perfectly planned schedule. If I nag him about these things, I chip away at the very traits that attracted me to him in the first place. I may get what I want—a more orderly, deliberate husband—but I also get what I don't want: a partner who is ordinary, predictable, and unhappy.

You fell in love because of the person your partner is. Reminding yourself of the essence of your mate's character will help you shrug off the small stuff.

Drama

A sharp tongue is the only edged tool that grows keener with constant use.

Washington Irving, "Rip van Winkle"

I have a sharp tongue, and I know how to use it. Once in a while, I hear myself say things that make my already-curly hair stand on end. My husband mostly takes my tirades in stride, sometimes just listening, sometimes cajoling me out of my mood, sometimes giving me a verbal cuff or two in return.

We must guard against turning the tool of language into a weapon against someone we love. Certainly there are times when our mate needs a talking-to. All I urge here is moderation—and taking a few moments to think before letting loose. Are we legitimately furious about the matter at hand, or are we lashing out about some hidden insult or hurt? Is there another way to handle the situation?

We cannot expect our partner to repair wrongs if we wrong our partner.

It's easier to be nasty than it is to be clear. Practice right action over acting out.

Good-bye, Hello

I shall light a candle of understanding in thine heart,
which shall not be put out.

2 Esdras 14:25 (The Apocrypha)

Working hard on separate projects, my husband and I haven't seen much of each other over the past few days. Yet when we finally reunite; we fight—when all we really want to do is enjoy each other.

Perhaps we are working off the tension of two coming together as one after operating largely solo all week. Perhaps we're disappointed to find that, even though they're the person we've longed to see, they still have all the warts that drive us crazy.

The only thing that helps is to remember that we didn't intend "hello" to be this way, and to start over, with feeling.

Separations confer both loneliness and freedom. It's natural for things to be rocky for a while afterward. Stay with it. It doesn't mean anything.

Healing Sleep

There is a time for many words, and there is also a
time for sleep.

Homer, *The Odyssey*

When my husband and I wake up in the morning, before either of us stirs, I notice we are breathing together, deep and long, in perfect synchrony. It is as if the night has wrought a small miracle of reattunement. Perhaps in the unconscious hours we spend sleeping, God somehow repairs the divisions the day creates. In just the way that wounds heal and tired muscles renew themselves in the night, it may be that sleeping together blesses us by reknitting our spirits.

Go to sleep touching each other. Partake of the healing of the night.

Drama, Scenes, Acts, and Plays

What manner of speech has escaped
the barrier of your teeth?

Homer, *The Iliad*

Sometimes we hold things in until we're furious. Then we make a scene. We may get the results we want, but the costs are high. No one has won when resentment smolders.

I have a habit of assuming that, without drama, I won't be listened to. Of course, there's no guarantee that stating my wishes calmly and clearly will get me my way. But for me, practicing moderation is not about getting what I want. Rather, it's a discipline in maintaining the steady conviction that I deserve to be heard; that I don't have to yell to make my points worth hearing. Even if I don't get the results I want, I have the satisfaction of knowing that I handled myself as I wanted to, not as I was compelled to.

Don't make scenes. Your voice will be heard better without them.

Stop Talking

. . .

Harpo Marx

Find a nonverbal way to communicate. Words aren't the only route to resolution. Touch preceded talk in our earliest life, and words can get us into trouble. There are times when we may still be hurting and wanting to make our point, yet we also crave the comradeship of the other person. If we talk about things in this tender state, the hot spots tend to flare up, and we'll be arguing again. At times like these, nonverbal connection can lead us out of the maze. It needn't be affectionate—at our house we stick our tongues out at each other ("You hurt me and I'm still mad, but I am ready to acknowledge your existence by sticking my tongue out at you."). It's juvenile, but then, so are many of our arguments. If we can admit this, we can reestablish contact and go forward together. Later, we may feel calm enough to talk things out from a place of unity, not angry isolation.

Reconnect with your hearts before you connect with words. Then, rebonded, apply your minds to the situation.

Attachment

I am a kind of burr; I shall stick.

William Shakespeare, *Measure for Measure*

It's unnerving to notice how attached I already am to my husband. When he's working hard and spending two or three evenings a week in his studio, I get sad, even a little weepy sometimes; suffering from the lack of his attention. I used to be ashamed of this. Here I was, a strong and independent woman with plenty of things to do, craving my husband's attention. Now I've decided it would be odd not to miss what I've spent thousands of hours nurturing. We're good together. We make each other happy. We calm each other down and stir each other up. We've labored for that deep knowledge of one another; worked hard to find and keep that edge of passion and solace. When I don't have it, I want it. That's good and natural.

Reaping the comfort of your hard work is half the fun of marriage.

Let Yourself Be Cared For

She brought forth butter in a lordly dish.

Judges 5:25

I'm sitting in my husband's art studio, eating the breakfast he has prepared of instant coffee and gingersnaps. We spent last night here, and this morning he's taking very good care of me, calibrating the temperature of my shower, letting me sleep twelve hours without interruption. Letting your partner take care of you is an act of generosity on both sides. It's important that your spouse feel indispensable to the fulfillment of your desires. People want to know that they make a difference. Allowing your partner to act on this human, noble desire to care for you is one simple, powerful way to do that.

When your partner cares for you, you are being given the gift of your lover's best self. Sink into it. We're lucky to have this very direct way to express our goodness to each other.

Resolution

Only when the year grows cold do we see that the pine and cypress are the last to fade.

Confucius, *Analects of Confucius*

Does it seem as though your conflicts become more difficult the longer you are married? Perhaps you are grappling with issues more deeply attached to your essential selves. You are pushing on each other's boundaries—and feeling secure enough to do so. It can be intimidating because the problems seem more convoluted, more intractable. You may wonder if you are losing your ability to communicate or compromise. I believe that when this happens we are growing to a new level of comfort with each other, one where we can wrestle longer and harder because we trust each other to persevere until an outcome is reached—or even if it is never reached.

When the problems get harder, it means you both feel safe enough to rock the boat—and strong enough to keep rowing even when there's no shore in sight.

Free to Go

"Nothing, so it seems to me," said the stranger, "is more beautiful than the love that has weathered the storms of life."

Jerome Klapka Jerome, *The Passing of the Third Floor Back*

Not a day goes by that you couldn't find a good reason to get divorced," my mother once told me. She and my father have been married for sixty years. After sixty years, are the "good reasons" still the same? It would be boring to have the same reasons; disheartening to have new ones. Yet I take comfort in her words, which promise me that a marriage can remain alive, full of static and connection, and that periodic thoughts of jumping overboard are unnatural only in their absence. What a relief! Now I can fantasize mutiny without fear that thinking equals doing. Marriage then becomes a choice, freely chosen, each day.

Knowing you can leave gives you the choice to stay. The open door is a sign of your commitment to remain.

Your Family and Friends

I have often regretted my speech, never my silence.

Publilius Syrus, Maxim 1070

Let your mate find his or her own way of relating to your family and friends. It's tempting to want to intervene, intermediate, make them like each other. This has much more to do with our need to integrate the varied spheres of our life than with helping the new relationship thrive. Introduce them, provide some backdrop of common ground—perhaps a topic that you know interests them both—and let them find their own footing. They've made the wary small talk of new acquaintances many times before. And they know what's at stake here. If they want to come together out of love for you, they will do so. If not, your prodding wishing, or pushing won't help.

Resist the urge to organize your spouse's experience of your friends and family members. They are grown-ups. As you love them, so you must trust them.

Your Partner's Family and Friends

Let each man have the wit to go his own way.

Sextus Propertius, *Elegies*

Sometimes it's difficult to establish a genuine way of connecting with our spouse's family or friends. It's hard to forge a unique connection, as we would normally do in friendship, because we are drawn into the role through our partner. If you are inclined, establish contact directly. Create your own unique relationship, outside the one with your spouse? Call to chat. Send a gift from you alone. Show the fullness of who you are so you can be understood on your own merits, not on what you represent or symbolize when occupying the role of spouse, stepparent, or in-law.

Don't let your spouse be the filter through which others experience you. Let people meet and see you on your own terms.

Share the Attraction

Come forth into the light of things.

William Wordsworth, "The Tables Turned"

Tell each other what you saw in one another when you first met. What was it about your true love that intrigued and attracted you? That crooked smile? That infectious laugh? Courteous behavior? Endearing diffidence? Quiet confidence? I remember my husband, on our second date, asking, "May I?" before he took my arm as we traversed an icy patch on the sidewalk. It was so unexpected—so sweetly courtly. I fell hard—and not on the ice.

It's nice to know what we saw in each other—it connects us to a time when the energy between us was thunderous, crackling with possibility.

Together, remember your common history. Sharing it with each other binds you together.

Creating Your Future

If thou follow thy star, thou canst not fail of a
glorious haven.

Dante, *The Divine Comedy*

Dreams for the future can be difficult to reconcile with the reality of the present. *How do we get from here to there?* we wonder. Dreams help a lifetime partnership flower—otherwise how could we have persevered through the rough patches? But when what we want seems too distant from what we have, the dissonance can feel unbearable. Some couples benefit from drawing up a plan; some by feeling their way through the organic process of living and changing. Or you may want to plan, while your partner wants to "flow"—or vice versa. A common ground to start from is the "now" you share and the fact that the two of you are all you have when more-transient trappings fall away. Work from this union, with your future union in mind.

In planning your future, whatever keeps you intact and growing, individually and together, is worth investigating.

What Silence Says

Foot-and-a-half-long words.

Horace, *Epistles*

While I'm writing this, my husband is in the kitchen washing the breakfast dishes. The radio and TV are off; the cat is sleeping among the windowsill plants. Companionable silence reigns.

There is something that bonds us in the quiet time we spend, not exactly apart, but not together, either. I think of us in these instances as gyrating companionably side by side, weaving our humble lives and growing a little older together. There's a sweetness to it; a sense of peaceful certainty. I see that we don't have to be doing things together in order to "be" together.

A marriage is built as much upon the quality of its silences as upon its conversations.

Sitting with Pain

The descent to Hades is the same from every place.

Anaxagoras, from Diogenes Laertius, *Lives of Eminent Philosophers*

Is there anything worse than knowing that you have dealt your relationship a lasting blow? Perhaps it was unpremeditated, delivered in a backhand slash when all your hurts, petty and otherwise, drew to a dagger point and you said something unforgettable. Now you can't take it back. You can usually tell when you've cut this deep because your partner goes silent. You have cut to the quick, past the point where anger can protect. You'll feel your partner's sadness at being disappointed in you.

We all want to be there for our spouse in bad times. It's painful to be there, however, when we realize that *we* are the bad time. Understand that even if able to forgive, your partner won't be able to forget. Sitting patiently with pain of your own making is the only thing you can offer now, after your sincere apology. At least show that although you can inflict pain, you are strong and loving and generous enough to live with its consequences.

Some hurts cannot be repaired, but at least they need not be endured alone.

Speak Up

For it is feeling and force of imagination that makes
us eloquent.

Quintilian, De *Institutione Oratoria*

Relationship experts exhort us to ask for what we want
from our partner; otherwise, how can our partner know
our desires? Many of us become pretty good at routing
requests: "Would you please clear the table?" "Can you pick
up cat food on your way home?" "Call if you're going to be
late." But why is it so hard to make out-and-out demands—
to say, "Stop that" or "Touch me here" or "For Valentine's
Day I would like flowers and to be taken out for dinner"?

Because we so desperately want to be understood, it's
tempting to make mind reading a criterion for true love. In
fact, true love is defined by your partner's ardent desire to
know and understand you in all your dimensions. Just as sharing your body is a conscious act of choice, so offering access
to your heart and mind must be, too.

**The willingness to open up—rather than wait to be
opened—is a hallmark of intimacy. It is the kind of
courage mature love demands.**

Holidays

If you wish to avoid foreign collision, you had better abandon the ocean.

Henry Clay, Speech in the House of Representatives, January 22, 1812

Holidays can challenge marriage. It can be difficult to be your real self when the family assembles. The pressures to fall into old roles and to create a "perfect" holiday combine to force us to do and be what we are not.

Rather than simply muddle through, set yourself up for better success by realizing that you can help each other maintain your real selves within the holiday hurly-burly. Or you can opt to get together with your family at other, less charged times. Working to remain genuine amid confusion involves staying in constant, gentle touch with the self. Be patient and applaud your progress, however incremental.

Holidays are not times to expect breakthroughs with family. Learn first how to manage yourself. The simple fact that you are acting different will begin to force a change in the family pattern.

The Real You

From childhood's hour I have not been / As others were—I have not seen / As others saw.

Edgar Allan Poe, "Alone"

Expect to play each other's parents in your marriage, and your own as well. Our parents were our first models for everything. It's natural that, when groping for ideas, we seize on the old, hardwired responses. You'll hear yourself say things you swore you'd never say. You'll discover your partner unwittingly casting you in the part of parent.

It's the moment when you feel most compelled to act a certain way that you must stop, question, and examine: What is the origin of this response? Do I stand by it? Does it reflect who I really want to be in my marriage?

You can also apply this inquiry in retrospect: How did you really want to handle things? Share your discoveries with your partner. Next time, perhaps both of you will be closer to the mark.

Becoming your true self in marriage takes time. Be patient, but keep stretching your wings.

Priorities

Ah! When will this long weary day have end,
And lend me leave to come unto my love?

Edmund Spencer, *Epithalamion*

Chores help us feel orderly, organized, and in control. They make for a smoother life. But trade them off with loving attention, and you risk an imbalance of priorities. There will always be more chores to do, and dust will conquer us all in the end. You have only your time on earth to love and be loved. Not all people are lucky enough to have the luxury of being loved. So do enough chores to be able to find your keys in the morning and your bed at night. Then remember what you were really put on earth to do: give and take your share in the cycle of love.

An orderly life is beside the point. Connection is the only real hedge against chaos.

Back Off

Great wisdom is generous; petty wisdom is contentious. Great speech is impassioned; small speech is cantankerous.

Chuang-tzu, "On Leveling All Things"

Sometimes a point is better made when not driven home. In the heat of the moment, you want to persist, push, make the outcome go your way. This can backfire if your partner ends up hearing your insistent voice but not your words. You're more likely to arrive at real resolution if you hold out for comprehension rather than insist on submission: "I'd rather talk than argue. Can we cool down and discuss this?" If you make room for your partner's point of view, your partner may give room to yours, both of you no longer cornered and compelled to defend your positions.

Respecting your partner's boundaries opens the way for your partner to respect yours.

A Gift

My true love hath my heart, and I have his.

Sir Philip Sidney, *The Arcadia*

Think of a person whom you respect highly. Now, place your partner above that person. The one who has chosen to spend his or her life with you deserves the highest respect you can give. We sometimes treat those closest to us the most carelessly, because we count on their commitment to keep them close to us. We need, instead, to see their love as the rare and fragile gift it really is. The fact that it's fragile doesn't mean that it isn't strong. It does mean that we have been entrusted with the most delicate, tender part of our partner. We must guard it well, for if we abuse our lover's love, we are abusing the greatest gift another can give, leaving him with nothing.

Your partner's love is a gift that need never have been given. Treat it—and your partner—accordingly.

Pick Your Prizes

Slight not what's near through aiming at what's far.

Euripides, *Rhesus*

Make a list of the things you want from your marriage. Then cross off half the entries. There are only so many things one can strive for. Decide on the items that are most important, and work on those. Build a marriage that satisfies you in several crucial ways, and hope for the best on the rest. It is better to come away with a few things finely honed than to end up with nothing in particular.

In marriage, there is no perfection. Expect some aspects of your union to be better than others.

Remember to Play

Let the world slide, let the world go;
A fig for care, and a fig for woe!

John Heywood, "Be Merry Friends"

Which of you is better at relaxing? Follow that person's lead whenever possible. We all know how to play. It's simply a question of allowing ourselves to remember what we already know.

Think about the things you do best and most happily together. Develop your daydreams until they're so real they won't be denied, compelling you to turn dreams into deeds. Enlist your partner's help in recalling shared good times. Remember how those times bonded you, wove your common history. The tapestry won't weave itself.

Take on your common dreams as projects. Weave them together. View your pleasures as being essential to your lasting partnership, not as things to pursue "when I have time." Recommit yourselves to playing together.

Play takes the lid off our joy. It unlocks the self our partner loves most.

Old Flames
and High Stakes

With you I should love to live,
with you be ready to die.

Horace, *Odes*

Old flames will flicker as long as the mind can consider what might have been. But you didn't choose the old flame, nor did your partner. You chose each other. You chose because you were ready for something more than transience. You sought transformation. A gift such as this naturally demands something in return: your daily presence—physical and emotional—in your marriage. Your marriage is only "there" to the extent that you are.

Don't wait for old flames to die. Instead, realize that both of you are playing in a much bigger game, for stakes that involve your very lives. Respect what each of you has willingly risked.

Play marriage as though your life depended on it.

Lost and Found

I wonder by my troth, what thou, and I
Did, till we lov'd?

John Donne, "The Good Morrow"

I think sometimes about what would happen if my husband died, suddenly and catastrophically. What frightens me is how I suspect I would fall apart, as though he were the trellis and I the vine. It's unnerving to feel this dependent. I like to feel effective, efficient, independent. I fight the scary sensation of merging that has gripped me so fast, so hard.

In truth, we're helpless against these feelings. We can't hold ourselves separate from our partner and feel intimate at the same time. Our job is much bigger and harder than that. Each of us must remain who we are, while losing ourselves in another.

In marriage, you are not you, and you are not not-you. You are a new entity altogether: a dynamic creation, becoming what you will be while remaining what you were.

Free to Be

**Most people live . . . in a very restricted circle of
their potential being.**

William James, *The Letters of William James*

I'm catching a cold," my husband announced on the morning
we were to embark on a trip. *Wait a minute*, I thought, *I'm the
one who gets sick on trips. He's not allowed to!*

It's upsetting when our spouse shows a characteristic that
we thought was reserved for us alone. We may feel peeved;
this isn't how our spouse is "supposed" to be: *He's* not allowed
to sulk when he's angry. *She's* not allowed to be captivating at
a party—only I am.

When did you start competing with each other for attention?

**Are you allowing each other to be all that you are? Are
you letting every dimension show?**

Oasis

With thee, in the Desert—
With thee in the thirst—
With thee in the Tamarind wood—
Leopard breathes—at last!"

Emily Dickinson, "No. 209"

Visiting with family can turn into an endless round of main events. It's easy to get caught up in the number of people to see and things to do, forgetting that you need time to return to yourselves for renewal and replenishment. Be sure to schedule some time for just the two of you to do a special activity. Perhaps it's a quiet breakfast at a sleepy café, a dodge into a dark movie theater, or an early-morning walk followed by companionable reading of the newspaper. Reconnect with yourselves as individuals and with each other as a couple.

When confusing surroundings threaten to pull you away from each other, take time to remember who you are.

Remember This

**The beginning is the most important
part of the work.**

Plato, *The Republic*

L ife can be too busy to allow time for making memories.
You are forging many firsts in these years together, firsts
that may become treasured family rituals. Keep a camera
handy; keep a journal of your travels; or make scrapbooks of
special mementos from times of special joy. You think you will
remember the details of these times, but you won't, not in all
their colors. Later, these memories of your early years will
become family keepsakes.

**These are important times. Make time for remembrances.
Consciously create a rich tapestry of shared history.**

Take a Break

To do two things at once is to do neither.

Publilius Syrus, Maxim 7

Did you think you could have all your "single" activities and a marriage, too? It's a myth that you can have it all, if only you could figure out how. Believe me, no one else is doing it nearly as well as they appear to be. Marriage takes effort. It fills your mind and your time. Some things are going to have to go by the wayside. You may later resume some activities while letting go of others. But don't exhaust yourself with wanting and trying to have everything. In partaking of many, you gain little from all.

Marriage takes, and takes hard. Make room for the energy it demands.

Coming Together

My morning incense, and my evening meal—
the sweets of Hasty Pudding.

Joel Barlow, "The Hasty Pudding"

My husband makes the pancake batter, using half the eggs called for by the recipe, the way he knows I like them. I set butter to soften atop the warm coffeemaker so he can have melted butter on his cakes, the way I know he likes them. We've developed our own unique recipe for spaghetti sauce that combines our separate tastes—thick and garlicky for him, bursting with mushrooms and onions for me. We shop separately and bring home treats for each other: the salt-free pretzels he likes; the salty corn chips I devour with salsa too hot for his taste.

We forge these traditions together, partly without realizing it, partly with the conscious wish to please each other. It's these little selfless acts and allowance for idiosyncrasies that make our union unique.

Celebrate the small ways in which you've created something very big that embraces you both.

Keeping It All Together

Practice and thought might gradually forge
many an art.

Virgil, *Georgics*

Are you getting what you need from your spouse most of the time? Are you providing to yourself those things for which you're responsible: your sense of your own goodness, your faith in the goodness of the world around you, your power to make a difference in your life and in the lives of others? Are you providing what your marriage requires, without losing yourself in the process? These are the paradoxical tasks of marriage: the simultaneous drawing of boundaries and bridges between you. You are not there to complete each other, yet you have a power together that you did not possess alone. You are not there to become each other, yet you experience a sensation of being one. Holding these opposing processes in balance takes enormous strength and energy. Expect wild seesawings sometimes.

Achieving balance in marriage is not a static state. It is an accumulation of thousands of adjustments, a continual correction of course.

Solo

From the great deep to the great deep he goes.

Alfred, Lord Tennyson, *Idylls of the King*, "The Passing of Arthur"

Some days you feel misunderstood, unappreciated, unseen by the person to whom you want to be most visible. There is no more desolate sensation. Only the remembrance of good times keeps you going—and the natural grit you are made of.

There are things about us our partner will never know, much less understand. We are all ultimately alone with ourselves. That is what makes the drive to bring another into our life so intense. It is filled with the ecstasy of finding someone in whom we see something of ourselves—and the pain of realizing that not even this person will ever really know us.

Loneliness is part of the human condition. Marriage does not banish it.

Interference

You'll find us rough, sir, but you'll find us ready.

Charles Dickens, *David Copperfield*

Sometimes my husband and I must make our points five or six times before we understand each other. We accuse each other of not listening, but in fact it's a simple problem of assuming that "he is me" and vice versa. After spending untold hours seeking commonalities and honing our shadows to fit together, we are in the habit of seeing ourselves reflected in our partner. When we're forced to notice our essential differences instead, we feel disoriented and lost. We blame the other for not "getting" us, when, in fact, what is taking place is a perfectly natural process of self-differentiation.

You don't need to be on the same wavelength to succeed in marriage. You just need to be able to ride each other's waves.

Your Partner's Wisdom

Minds are like parachutes. They only function when
they are open.

Sir James Dewar

"His wife's really jealous," my husband said about a friend's
spouse. "I told him, 'You've got to handle that right
away. You can't just let it go. It's a basic issue that's not going
to disappear.'"

Don't underestimate your partner's ability to see clearly
what ails a marriage. After all, would you have married
someone you considered clueless? How your partner arrives
at these insights may be a mystery to you, but something's
always cooking in your mate's consciousness, be sure of that.
It's worth it to quiet your own mind and watch and wait for
your partner's wisdom.

**The more preposterous you think your partner's ideas are,
the more unique sense they probably contain. They reveal
to you the mystery you married.**

Accept Doubts

It was, of course, a grand and impressive thing to do,
to mistrust the obvious, and to pin one's faith in
things which could not be seen!

Galen, *On the Natural Faculties*

There is a part of me that holds back in my marriage; a part that says, "What would happen if all this disappeared tomorrow?" This is the part of me that doesn't believe our best efforts will prevail; that wants to keep the lines of demarcation ("that's yours, and this is mine") sharply drawn.

I don't know whether to resist this instinct or to heed it. Is this a voice of irrational fear that should be ignored? Or is it a voice of reason, shunning the merge-everything attitude toward marriage that can be so dangerous to the survival of self?

I can only grope through this by asking in each instance: "Do I feel unsafe, in any way, by doing this?" If the answer is yes, then I must heed that warning or risk being less than honest with myself and my partner.

For your own sake and for the sake of your full presence in your marriage, listen to all the conversations within, no matter how disturbing.

Getting and Spending

A feast is made for laughter, and wine maketh
merry: but money answereth all things.

Ecclesiastes 10:19

Money may be handled in different ways at different times in your marriage. Much depends on who is earning more of it, whether there are imbalances in how (and by whom) it is being spent, and the amount of trust and power you accord each other in financial matters. As trust and power levels shift, and as the economic balance between you changes, expect questions of money to arise. Assume there will be discussions—sometimes heated. Be aware of resentment about money/power issues leaking into other areas of your life together. This is a balance that may need frequent fine-tuning.

In our culture, money symbolizes everything from power to comfort. Expect its issues to appear in your marriage in many different guises.

Your Basic Fights

"I am not an angel," I asserted; "...you must neither
expect nor exact anything celestial of me—for you
will not get it, any more than I shall get it of you:
which I do not at all anticipate."

Charlotte Brontë, *Jane Eyre*

Oh yeah, we have our dog/housework argument once a
week," my friend said with a chuckle. That's about as
often as my husband and I have our newspaper/clutter
argument. Much of the madness of marriage is each person's
persistence in doing what they want despite the other's
energetic efforts to get them to do otherwise. You make room
for each other the way prizefighters move aside to pass in the
narrow hallway outside the ring. There's no graciousness to it;
only a narrow-lipped tolerance.

**After marriage, only a few things really change in our
habits and behaviors. Go for the important ones, and
expect to keep battling off and on about the rest. It's
okay. You can fight a lot without it meaning anything,
good or bad, about your marriage.**

Play, Pleasure, Frolic, and Fun

If you have two loaves of bread,
sell one and buy a hyacinth.

Persian saying

Free time is called that for a reason. What you do during free time should make you feel free. What untethers you may not be what untethers your mate. Neither of you should clip the other's wings, nor make chores your main hobby. No one was ever barred from heaven for having ring around the collar. Heaven rewards integrity, and you can't have integrity without being integrated in all your parts: not just in how you relate to others, but also in how you relate to yourself; not just in how well you work, but also in how reverently you receive pleasure.

Revere your free time and use it joyfully. You cannot give from an empty cup.

The Unknown

"The whole difference between construction and creation is exactly this: that a thing constructed can only be loved after it is constructed; but a thing created is loved before it exists."

Gilbert Keith Chesterton, in "The Pickwick Papers,"
Appreciations and Criticisms of the Works of Charles Dickens

Each of us has a responsibility to carry our own frailties. We honor our partner by confiding our burdens selectively, not dumping them. We are not children anymore, believing we can hand over fears and transgressions to an all-loving, all-giving parent.

The paradoxical challenge of marriage is to approach it with all the ebullient hope of the child and all the hard-won wisdom of experience. This means holding our responsibilities on our own shoulders, being accountable for our own life, uniting ourselves with our partner, not by deluging each other with our pasts, but by shaping our common future with conscious, careful hands.

True partnership is measured not by how well you know each other but by how well you create yourselves together.

Keep Learning

**Draw from others the lesson
that may profit yourself.**

Terence, *Heauton Timorumenos*

Talk about other people's marriages—not as a point of gossip or self-comparison, but as a point of departure in discovering where the two of you stand on a given issue. Doing this gives you the opportunity to discuss your marriage in the abstract, without the emotional tension of a specific conflict charging the conversation. Notice a couple's positives. ("I like how they play off of each other, building on each other's ideas.") Notice something that puzzles you. ("Do you notice how quiet and sad Fred seems when Sally is talking? I wonder what's going on there.") Let others teach you about yourselves.

Watch marriage at work in others. Learn those lessons together.

Fits and Starts

Improvement makes straight roads; but the crooked
roads without improvement are roads of genius.

William Blake, *The Marriage of Heaven and Hell*, "Proverbs of Hell"

When we seek improvement in our marriage, we probably know better than to expect it to be immediate. What we may not know is that, once it happens, it isn't permanent. Change is like the universe: Randomness is its organizing principle. As suddenly as new behavior arrives, just as suddenly it takes its departure. As with any skill newly learned, proficiency progresses in fits and starts as we struggle to master the details.

Have patience with the transient appearance of improvements. Much is being moved forward on many fronts. Understand that both of you are doing the best you can right now.

Compromise

Do not move the markers
on the border of the fields.

Amenemope, *The Instruction of Amenemope*

Compromise isn't wise if you're going to be mad about it. Folks will tell you that marriage is about compromise, but I think it has more to do with defining what you're not willing to compromise on, knowing that if you do compromise, you will take your dissatisfaction out on your spouse, one way or another. Understanding the subtleties of your inner wiring is where marital maturity resides. Anyone can give up and give in. Not everyone can listen to the clamor within and come up with a sane, considered response that answers your needs as well as the demands of the situation.

The work of marriage is not in compromise. It's in careful judgment, day by day, of where you end and your partner begins. Work gently with yourself in finding your way on this path.

Slipups

We live, not as we wish to, but as we can.

Menander, *Lady of Andros*

We begin marriage with the best of intentions. The busy-ness of life tends to strain those intentions, however, and suddenly we realize how long it's been since we did, said, or thought the ideals we started with. Then it's up to us to bring ourselves back to our original purpose.

Think of an area where your behavior has lagged of late. Observe what you do without censure: "I notice how critical I am of my partner. I will work on reframing the way I say negative things." Then, as you go about your days, keep that one goal in mind. When you hear yourself sliding into old habits, gently correct course.

Perfection is not the goal. The reward is in the learning of the caring vigilance that sustains the life lived consciously.

Beyond Being Heard

The way of a fool is right in his own eyes.

Proverbs 12:15

We spend a lot of time in marriage trying to make ourselves understood. We explain, demonstrate, explain again. Frequently what gets us into arguments is our frustration at not feeling understood. The discussion can often degenerate into each side stubbornly trying to hammer home its message—unless you make a conscious effort to stand for something larger than the point you desperately want to make.

Beyond being heard and being right, what is the "partnership benefit" of resolving the issue between you?

Let It Pass

Love truth, but pardon error.

Voltaire, "Le Mondain"

When your partner makes a dumb mistake, let it pass. Think about it: Do you like having your nose rubbed in your deficiencies? Such scrapes to the ego seem minor, but they accrue over time and mar the atmosphere between you. For minor transgressions innocently committed and soon regretted, you'll heal the breach sooner with understanding than with recriminations.

Practice forgiveness in your marriage. Both of you will need its favors.

The Fire between You

Love is a spirit all compact of fire,
Not gross to sink, but light, and will aspire.

William Shakespeare, *Venus and Adonis*

Your passion for each other is the source of sexual ecstasy, deep rage, and rapt hope. The fire between you fuels all energy, good and bad. Trying to extinguish negative energy between you will dampen other fires, too. Resignation in place of resolution removes all hope from marriage. To be conflict-free should not be the goal. Perhaps the aim should be to tend the fire better, rather than throw sand on the flames.

The problem may lie not in the marriage itself, but in the quality of the care it receives.

Planned Surprises

Variety is the soul of pleasure.

Aphra Behn, *The Rover*

We meet like lovers on the sly: my husband biking home from softball practice; me sitting on a certain park bench I know he'll pass. There's a shock of recognition; a smile of pleasure; a warmth in his eyes that says he likes this setup just fine.

It's all part of finding ways to make our relationship new, introducing the unknown when so much has become known. We tacitly agree to surprise each other in carefully orchestrated ways: to look the other way while one of us packs a birthday picnic, disappears down a bookstore aisle and reappears with a package under one arm, or tosses a gift catalog our way and casually asks which items we like.

As your marriage ripens, you'll adopt such little tricks. The fact that both of you know it is half the fun: It shows that each of you is committed to keeping romance alive. Is there any greater aphrodisiac?

Plan surprises. Give each other room to create newness between you.

Odyssey to Joy

Come live with me, and be my love; / And we will all
the pleasures prove / That valleys, groves, hills, and
field, / Woods or steepy mountain yields.

Christopher Marlowe, "The Passionate Shepherd to His Love"

We're inching down a cliff at Nevada Falls in Yosemite Valley. Beside us roars a white sheet of water. The descent is nearly trailless. We slide from rock to rock, sunburned and thirsty, shivering in the draft of the freezing water.

"I'm scared," I whine, sliding on my rear. "I'm tired. I can't!"

"Come *on!*" my husband yells, rushing ahead. "We're almost at the Mist Trail. You can't miss the Mist Trail!"

He had already climbed and descended this trail once. He had come back to get me, determined that I should see what he had seen. Without his persistence, I never would have made a memory to last a lifetime: gazing up into a wall of water, soaked and triumphant, and seeing three perfect circular rainbows in the mist.

Marriage is often about persisting in the face of our partner's resistance. We are vow-bound never to stop trying.

Sometimes we kick and scream all the way to exultation.

Who's Got the Problem?

Now 'tis the spring, and weeds are shallow-rooted;
Suffer them now and they'll o'ergrow the garden.

William Shakespeare, *King Henry VI, part 1*

When we're doing things in our marriage that aren't healthy for us, it's tempting to blame our partner rather than own up to our part in the matter. If you're doing the laundry for the umpteenth time and furious at your spouse for not sharing the task, ask yourself, *Who expected me to do this?* It sometimes happens that we are the ones expecting these things from ourselves. In your life together, which complaints are yours to own?

Identify some behaviors that don't work for you anymore. Clear them out, like old crabgrass.

Positive Complaints

*The final cause, then, produces motion
through being loved.*

Aristotle, *Metaphysics*

My husband is a night owl, surfing the airwaves for late-night talk shows and old B movies. Invariably I'm asleep long before he falls into bed. For a long time, I nagged him to come to bed earlier, citing all sorts of reasons ranging from healthfulness to savings on the electric bill. Then it occurred to me that it wasn't much fun for him to be badgered like this. Besides, I realized, I wasn't telling him the truth. It wasn't that I found fault with his night-owl ways (as my comments implied). I just missed him and wanted him next to me. So now I say, "Hey, come to bed. I miss you." It doesn't always work, but that's beside the point. What I want is love and attention, which I promptly receive. And there's no more nagging at bedtime.

Does your partner know the positive reasons behind your complaints?

A Promise

Promise is most often given when the least is said.

George Chapman, *Hero and Leander*

Once in a while, a conflict in marriage challenges us to the very end of our endurance. We feel we just can't take it another minute. We must escape this embattled place; find cool, free air. Where does the strength come from to hold the course, to stay, to take a breath and press on; to dig deep and find in ourselves one more minute, and the next, and the next?

Sometimes only a thin, strong thread ties us to our original commitment to each other: We stay because we said we would. It is the power of our word that keeps us there, not because we want to be, need to be, or know what to do. We stay because we promised. That is a scary place—a place bare of toeholds, stripped of ornament. That is a lonely place, for our partner is not there with us, but is clinging, alone, to a separate cliff.

There are moments in marriage when you will wonder how to endure. Remember that while you are wondering, you are enduring. Trust your power to cling to the rock when all the ropes have been cut.

Solace

A small rock holds back a great wave.

Homer, *The Odyssey*

Watch a toddler climb into his mother's lap for comfort, and be assailed by the wish to be held, to disappear behind someone's protective arms. We all need this holding time when we can feel safe and free, for a few minutes, from our responsibilities. Provide plenty of this to each other. It's not weak to seek comfort. Only the strongest among us can admit we need it.

Give and take comfort often. Make it physical, enveloping. Help each other shut out the world.

Ways of Giving

Well roared, Lion.

William Shakespeare, *A Midsummer Night's Dream*

Your partner's gifts to the marriage will not be the same as yours. They will be all his or her own, formed by personal skills, interests, and the unique construction of love for you. It's easy to value your own contributions to the relationship—the sacrifice and selflessness of these are easy for you to see. It's more challenging to view your partner's contributions in light of what they mean to your partner, rather than through the lens of your own values. Remember, your mate has a vested interest in making this marriage work. Your mate, like you, is trying.

Notice the differences in how the two of you work at your marriage. Rather than focusing on what you want, try focusing on what your partner gives.

Exits and Entrances

For God's sake hold your tongue, and let me love.

John Donne, "The Canonization"

You need reentry time. So does your spouse. Even when making as simple a transition as the daily arrival home from work, give each other space to unwind, regroup, rethink yourselves into the next sequence of action. Create a homecoming ritual that both of you enjoy. Maybe you always take a moment to kiss—really kiss—hello. Perhaps you share a glass of wine and talk about the day. Perhaps you cuddle together on the bed for a few minutes. Figure out what each of you needs to do in order to enter the evening as a whole, fully present person. Then provide this to each other.

No one can do the day without a break. Give this to each other as an act of kindness.

No Perfect Fits

**Where can we find two better hemispheres
Without sharp North, without declining West?**

John Donne, "The Good Morrow"

Life is filled with asymmetries—consider rocks, trees, the patterns of waves. Organic matter achieves a paradoxical constancy in this. Since we are organic matter, we should expect asymmetries between ourselves and should never expect perfect union. A perfect thing couldn't survive the changeability of its environment.

Perhaps the incongruences between you are like the asymmetries that make nature so resilient in the face of disaster. Perhaps, rather than trying to file down your rough edges so you can make a perfect fit, it is better to examine how the differences between you push you to new learnings, new strivings, new understandings never achieved on your own.

Perhaps it's your incompatibilities that help you to thrive.

Strangers

The human heart has hidden treasures,
In secret kept, in silence sealed.

Charlotte Brontë, "Evening Solace"

After much busyness that keeps you apart and pre-occupied, are you startled to find yourselves with open time together? Without the daily minutiae of duties, news, and gossip to exchange, are you casting about for conversation? This can be unsettling, so much so that it's tempting to avoid instances that bring you simply together, with nothing to do. Don't shy away. It's natural to feel at a loss at first. It doesn't mean you are growing apart or any other significant thing. It just means that the world is too much with you and you need time to shift gears, to enter a quieter, more subtle level with each other. Give yourselves time to adjust to a slower tempo.

Sit quietly with your unease with each other. The process of reacquaintance takes its own time.

Altruism

Great thoughts come from the heart.

Luc de Clapiers, Marquis de Vauvenargues, *Reflexions et Maximes*

Not long ago, my husband presented me with a small box of watercolors. "So you can paint on our trip to New Mexico," he said. Later he noticed a newspaper ad for a sale at our local bookstore. Three times he asked me, "Is there any book I can get for you?" Yesterday he left on my nightstand a yoga book he had bought some years back. "You said your back was tense. I thought this might help."

One miracle of marriage is that we discover in ourselves and in our partner a true desire to help the other person become his or her best self. I think it is the part of us that is most noble, even the most godly, because it is about creating—not in our own image, but in the image of God we see in one another. It is love that draws this from us: an intimation of the divine pushing us to realize our potential and to help our partner to do the same. Treasure and nurture these impulses as gifts of God, calling you toward the life you were meant to live.

Generosity is you, leaving yourself. Ecstasy has the same impulse.

Boasting, Bragging, and Praising

Through desire a man, having separated himself,
seeketh and intermeddleth with all wisdom.

Proverbs 18:1

How often do you brag about each other? I'm talking about the proud sharing of accomplishments or deeds or talents that lets others know the deep respect you hold for each other. Do you admire one another, not for how well you complement each other, but for the very differentness between you; the ways in which you are each unique and complementary wholly unto yourselves?

Think about what makes your partner unusual, someone to be noticed and honored. If you find yourself reluctant to give praise publicly, there's often a private power struggle going on. Search it out.

Be alert to the nagging reluctances that tug you away from each other. They mean more than you think.

Handling You

"Well, what does she want then?" said the flounder.
"Ah, flounder," said he, "my wife wants to be
Emperor."

Grimm's Fairy Tales, "The Fisherman and His Wife"

Sometimes we act dreadfully. Our spouse puts up with it. All of us have blind spots that keep us from governing ourselves when it might do us the most good. Our partner just stands there, right in the path of the hurricane. That anyone would choose to stand there at all is a wonder. That our mate jumps into the gale with us is a testimony to the bravery love spawns. Let your partner give you a reality check when you need it. It may be the last thing you want to hear, but it could be the only thing that gets through.

Sometimes we need to be set straight.

Feel It All

He who doesn't lose his wits over certain things has no wits to lose.

Gotthold Ephraim Lessing, *Emilia Galotti*

To feel life's joys deeply is also to feel its jagged edges. If we are sentient people, we can't escape feeling frayed at times by the force of our emotions. Days or weeks may pass when nothing seems right between us and our partner, and all we can do is hang in there and wait it out. Any truly passionate relationship contains the full complement of emotions, from fury to tenderness that passes all understanding. You have to be a little crazy in order to be able to take it all standing up. Don't worry when things look dark. It is only one part of the spectrum.

Expect bad patches. You can only "lose it" if you've found it.

Between the Lines

All poetry is difficult to read,
The sense of it is, anyhow.

Robert Browning, *The Ring and the Book*

Poetry is the language of excision: As much is said in what's left out as in what is included. Your partner is like a poem—epigrammatic, filled with nuance and unknowns, going at things slantwise. It's unrealistic to expect to read any poem with linear clarity. The richness is in what is unsaid or half-known. You will read your lover for years and learn something different every time. That makes for interest over the long haul. It also means that you must forgive yourself for not "getting it" all right away.

We are poems personified: our truths are revealed layer by layer, over the course of many readings.

Choose the Positive

To him who is in fear, everything rustles.

Sophocles, *Acrisius*

When I look for trouble in my marriage, I can always find it. Familiarity can lull us into expecting certain negatives in our partner. If we seek them, they will be there—along with a host of others we're all too primed to see. This is not to say that we must play the cockeyed optimist, blind to flaws. It does mean that focusing on the negative is our choice to make. And the more we look, the more we will see. Why not assume that the same could be true of our partner's positive traits, and focus on those instead?

Resist the pull toward the negative. Give the positive equal time.

Keep Going

To dry one's eyes and laugh at a fall,
And baffled, get up and begin again.

Robert Browning, "Life in a Love"

Bafflement is a big part of marriage. Continuing despite confusion is the strength you must apply. Often you'll have no clear idea why you're arguing, worrying, or feeling sad. It only gets clearer with time. And time's enlightenment can happen only if you get up, baffled, and return to the journey. Don't stand there in your puddle, insisting that the rain stop, before you move on. You will get wet either way, but if you start walking you'll at least be getting somewhere. Sometimes the act of moving on is itself a step toward understanding.

Keep moving, despite confusion. The learnings are in the going.

'Til Death

**The ring, so worn as you behold,
So thin, so pale, is yet of gold.**

George Crabbe, "His Mother's Wedding Ring"

"Do I know?" the old man in the wheelchair quavers, staring up at the trees through his giant sunglasses. "I don't know what I know, and I don't know what I don't know."

His wife sits near him on a park bench, her hand covering his where it lies strapped to the arm of his wheelchair. "You know my friend Rose?" she asks, trying to start a conversation. "Do I *know*?" he repeats. And the litany starts again.

I hope I will have the strength, should the time come, to show the tender patience this woman shows her husband, who barely recognizes her. It's hard to think that our decades together might end with one of us slowly slipping out of reach. The idea that we may have to watch each other die as part of our life partnership is barely conceivable. Watching elderly lovers care for each other shows so very clearly what it really means to commit for life.

Marriage never ends. Not ever.

Choose Your Attitude

The universe is change; our life is what our thoughts make it.

Marcus Aurelius Antoninus, *Meditations*

If both of us are cranky, one of us has to un-crank," my friend says of her marriage. Do you work at sending out good energy in your marriage? In a tense situation, do you ever make a conscious decision to reverse the thrust and create positive momentum rather than let conflict take over? It takes maturity, and an eye on the ball, to recognize that although we have the choice to keep making our point over and over, it is braver to select a different path to meet our ends. Choice opens new possibilities in marriage. It invites us out of our rut.

Attitude shapes action, and attitude is a choice, freely made, every day.

Losing Yourself vs. Letting Go

Facts which at first seem improbable will, even on
scant explanation, drop the cloak which has hidden
them and stand forth in naked and simple beauty.

Galileo Galilei, *Dialogues concerning Two New Sciences*

It is essential to hold on to your personal hopes, dreams, and
desires in marriage. It's also instructive, sometimes, to throw
your agenda to the wind—not in order to bow to your partner's
wishes, but to see what possibilities open up when you remove
the blinders that focus you on what you've decided is
important. Perhaps you'll discover new, unthought-of goals to
pursue, having given yourself the space in which to see them.
Perhaps you'll find a more inventive way to pursue both
personal and mutual aims. Look for ways to move outside
yourself and claim a wider sphere.

**Drop your focus from time to time to see if having it still
feels good.**

Family Identity

I don't believe there's no sich a person!

Charles Dickens, *Martin Chuzzlewit*

Your spouse knows you as a grown-up. Your family, however, may treat you more like the child you were than the adult you have become. Your spouse's behavior toward you can help remind your family that you are an adult, complete with opinions, ideas, skills, and dreams of your own. In this way, you and your partner can support each other when it comes to dealing with family—not by fronting for one another, but by treating one another like the adults you are. Seeing a spouse's respectfulness, deference, and protectiveness can be a powerful reminder to family members that yours has become a relationship of equals.

When you are with family, continue to be yourselves with each other.

Trial by Tempest

Give me a spirit that on this life's rough seas
Loves t'have his sails filled with a lusty wind,
Even till his sail-yards tremble, his masts crack,
And his rapt ship run on her sails so low
That she drinks water, and her keel plows air.

George Chapman, *The Conspiracy of Charles, Duke of Byron*

You never know if your boat will sink until you sail it on the open sea. Have you built her solidly, using the best seaworthy materials? Do you keep her lovingly, so that what began strong remains so?

The strength of your marriage is tested by how it floats over time, on seas both rocky and smooth. Hitting rough weather quickly shows you where the weak spots are. Storms give you a chance to plug the holes. Storms aren't personal; they don't judge you as being good if you survive or bad if you don't. They are simply opportunities to sail your boat with courage and pride.

If a storm comes up, ride into it and let it really rock. Storms show us that we can survive and find our way to calmer seas.

Basic Information

Though marriage makes man and wife one flesh, it
leaves 'em still two fools.

William Congreve, *The Double Dealer*

I don't like getting up in the morning. I doze and delay, groan
and grouse, until the last possible moment. When I try to
catch those few extra minutes of delicious sleep, my husband
warns, "You're going to be late for work! Come *on*, get up!"
This never makes me move any faster. It just makes me grumpy.

Finally, one day, I had an epiphany: "He thinks he's helping me. I've never explained that this is not how I need to be
helped." So the next time the cycle started, I gave him
acknowledgment rather than annoyance ("Honey, I appreciate
your helping me get up so I won't feel rushed and be late for
work") and *information* ("But, you know, it would help me a
lot more if you would just snuggle up with me for a few minutes to help me wake up a little more, and not mention getting up at all"). "Oh!" was his response. "Well, why didn't you
say so?"

**Without information, our partner has no way to make
improvements.**

Sex Talks

Full nakedness! All joys are due to thee,
As souls unclothed, bodies unclothed must be,
To taste whole joys.

John Donne, "To His Mistress Going to Bed"

"Sex is a very fine way of communicating," a friend confided. "When I'm not attracted to my husband, it means there's something to be discussed."

When something has blocked the flow of energy between you, the stress may first show up in the delicate channels of your sexual response. Rather than work at sex, it may be more productive to work on the problem. The best route may be simple honesty and curiosity: "We haven't made love in weeks. I miss you. What's going on?" Patiently get to the bottom of whatever needs to be talked about. When the sexual channel opens, you'll know that healing has begun.

Don't let your problems sleep with you. Your bed should be just big enough for two.

Staying Connected

Time takes all and gives all.

Giordano Bruno, *The Candle Bearer*

I watch an older couple in a restaurant. Their entire meal passes without one word between them. They stare at their plates, at other diners, into space—anywhere but at each other. *Where did the intense involvement, the obsession, of courtship go? I wonder. Must it end in this bland soup of indifference?*

I believe there is another way, where the passion of the beginning becomes a kind of psychic sympathy—an understanding beyond words—that allows you to anticipate each other's need for bread, pepper, silence, talk. It lets you see, without looking, the image of the other. It has nothing to do with the exhaustion of familiarity; everything to do with the focused transmutation of the explosive energy that fuels every couple's beginning. That is the energy I want to keep forever.

Every day you can either lose or find each other. Work your connection like a muscle.

A Thought's Power

Strong is the soul, and wise, and beautiful;
The seeds of god-like power are in us still;
Gods are we, bards, saints, heroes, if we will!

Matthew Arnold, "Written in Emerson's Essays"

I don't ever want to lose sight of the fact that my husband is my lover," a woman told me. "As soon as I think of him as my dowdy old spouse, I'm sure that's what he'll think of me."

Our thoughts about our marriage shape our partner as much as they shape us. The bond between you is so close, so much like a membrane; expect attitudes to travel between you no less than words. If you are dissatisfied, consider that you may not be the only one having those feelings. Feelings are contagious. They move between you, shaping you together and separately. Respect the power of attitudes to sculpt behavior, and handle them with care.

What you think is who you become.

Same Old Story?

Indeed he knows not how to know who knows not also how to un-know.

Sir Richard Francis Burton, *The Kasidah of Haji El-Yazdi*

Have you heard many of your partner's stories before? Instead of tuning out, consider what the story reveals about your partner. Each of us creates a kind of mythology of our lives, construing events and circumstances according to the meaning they hold for us. The stories we repeat the most often are those that we have invested with the most profound significance. What do your partner's stories tell you about his or her hopes, dreams, and ideas about how life ought to be?

Listen to your partner with ears attuned to something beyond words.

Found Moments

Five miles meandering with a mazy motion.

Samuel Taylor Coleridge, "Kubla Kahn"

By chance we find ourselves with a Saturday free of chores, errands, and obligations. We spend the morning in the West Village, poking around in old bookstores, perusing the contents of our favorite collective shops. We discover a tidy little coffee bar where neighborhood folks lounge on benches outside, drinking caffe latte and flipping through the newspaper. We linger two hours over cappuccino and scones, engrossed in the best conversation we've had in weeks.

Make room in your marriage for the pleasure of the unexpected. Plan time with no plans, where these small moments of impromptu magic can happen. These are the moments that unite and comfort you—and that will become shining prisms in your common memory.

Marriage is built on its details.

Just You Two

If ever two were one, then surely we.
If ever man were loved by wife, then thee;
If ever wife was happy in a man,
Compare with me ye women if you can.

Anne Bradstreet, "To My Dear and Loving Husband"

We travel on the train, returning from a weekend with other couples. It's been fun but busy, and we hold hands and doze as the train speeds us back to familiar life one-on-one. We are glad to be alone again; glad to be "just us" again; happy in the silences we create together, in which we dream or just lie back, thinking of nothing much at all.

The next time you have been out socializing, note the moments when you rejoin each other, just the two of you. It is a gift to have friends and a thrill to be with them. But there is a glowing contentment, a serene awareness, that comes from the times when you return, exhilarated from your travels, to the cocoon you two have made.

Feel the contrast between the world outside and the one you inhabit as a couple. Return to each other often for rest and renewal.

Purity

Manifest plainness,
Embrace simplicity,
Reduce selfishness,
Have few desires.

Lao-tzu, *The Way of Lao-tzu*

There are few clearer words than these to describe the highest goals to seek in marriage. When plainness fosters truth in word and deed; when simplicity manifests in easy, straightforward communication; when selfishness and desire are set aside so both of you may work for the marriage rather than for the self, there opens up a path you can take to find each other—a fellow striver who is your partner.

Marriage flourishes in the light of pure intentions.

Celebrate Yourselves

And we meet, with champagne and a chicken, at last.

Lady Mary Wortley Montagu, *The Lover*

Today is our anniversary: a time to consider how far we've come and how far we're going. Strangely, we have to keep reminding ourselves to celebrate. Making a big deal about our anniversary feels a little odd—as if we had suddenly decided to lionize our arms or legs. Seeing our marriage as existing apart from us is a foreign exercise.

Not surprisingly, we come up dry of ideas for fancy com-memorations. Finally, we end up doing what we do so well together: hanging out. At a nearby Mexican restaurant, we feast on green chile enchiladas and share a beer—a habit we got into on a recent trip to the Southwest. We talk, laugh, walk home arm in arm, just like we always do. The evening is exactly what an anniversary should be: a celebration of what we treasure.

You have a natural reverence for each other. Let yourselves be guided by your own lights.

Afterword: Looking Back and Forward

As I put the finishing touches on the fourth incarnation of this book and recall that I began writing the original edition just after my first anniversary, I ponder how it holds up to my experiences now, as a married woman of almost twelve years.

Remembering those days when I got up early to "go write epiphanies," as my husband sleepily called them, I realize that while I came to my marriage with what I consider a highly evolved set of operating principles for relationships, spending a small amount of time each day simply thinking about what marriage means to me allowed me to create a much more fully developed "marriage mind-set" than I otherwise would have had. And I can confirm now what I could only hope then: that with these principles at least formulated, if not always perfectly practiced, I had a basis for making a marriage that has lasted.

I also realize in reading these pages that, alongside the depth bestowed by time and shared experience in a maturing marriage, there are also the risks of habituation: habits of relationship I need to reinvigorate; habits of thinking I have gotten stuck in; habits of hurried communication. These wrap around a marriage like vines on a tree, sapping sustenance and hampering growth. In short, it's all too easy to go on automatic pilot in marriage.

With this insight comes understanding that the purpose of the book still rings true: Through the relatively mild discipline of thinking a bit each day about the meaning of marriage, there is a way to bring more consciousness and care to daily interactions, adding up to a whole that's immeasurably rich.

Marriage doesn't demand that we do it perfectly, but that we consider it, respect it, and continue to try. I continue to hope. I continue to laugh. I continue to trust that my husband is doing his best most of the time, and so am I.

My wish for you is that this book will bring you insights into your relationship habits, a hardy perspective that looks honestly at yourself as well as your partner, and the humor to take the entire endeavor both more and less seriously.

Finally, I share below a series of guidelines that you may find contradictory, which is precisely the point. Some days one will work; other days you'll need to go with its opposite. And that is just as it should be—must be—in any adventure undertaken for life. Isn't the fact that things can always change the most hopeful prospect you can imagine?

- Agree with your partner on how you're going to "do" your marriage. No one else's opinion matters.

- When you're proven wrong, admit it aloud.

- When you're proven right, don't rub it in.

- Be glad your partner will call you on your shenanigans—who else will bother?

- When you complain to someone about your partner, be aware that you're talking to the wrong person.

- When life between you is good, remember what you were doing to make it good.

- When life between you is not good, start doing what you did when things were good.

- Insist sometimes on getting your way.

- Let your partner have his or her way equally often.

- Be willing now and then to say "I'm sorry" even when you've done nothing wrong.

- Give your partner at least one compliment every day, no matter what.

- When you're about to lose your temper, ask a civil question.

- Struggle always means something—but not always what you think.

- Be proud of yourselves.

- Make some kind of skin-to-skin contact each day, no matter what.

- Have "inside" jokes.

- Do not address any important issue when you're hungry.

But perhaps all these words can be summed up by Henry James: "Three things in human life are important. The first is to be kind. The second is to be kind. And the third is to be kind."

Blessings and joy on your journey.

Index

Capitalized entries and bold-face page numbers denote meditations.

About the Author

Curtis Cowles

Toni S. Poynter is the author of *From This Day Forward*, featured in *Glamour*, the *Chicago Tribune*, on *Good Day New York*, and elsewhere. A veteran book editor for more than 20 years, she speaks on publishing topics at such venues as the American Society of Journalists and Authors (ASJA), New York University School of Continuing Education, and writers' conferences. She is a member of the Authors Guild, the Women's Media Group, and Women in Publishing and serves on the Executive Committee of the Books for a Better Life Awards. Currently a senior editor at HarperCollins Publishers, she lives with her husband in New York City.